KU-736-584

Venepuncture and Cannulation
A practical guide

Nicola Brooks

Venepuncture and Cannulation: A practical guide
Nicola Brooks

ISBN: 978-1-905539-44-4

First published 2014

All rights reserved. No part of this publication may be reproduced, stored in a retrieval system, or transmitted in any form or by any means, electronic, mechanical, photocopying, recording or otherwise, without either the prior permission of the publishers or a licence permitting restricted copying in the United Kingdom issued by the Copyright Licensing Agency, 90 Tottenham Court Road, London, W1T 4LP. Permissions may be sought directly from M&K Publishing, phone: 01768 773030, fax: 01768 781099 or email: publishing@mkupdate.co.uk

Any person who does any unauthorised act in relation to this publication may be liable to criminal prosecution and civil claims for damages.

British Library Cataloguing in Publication Data

A catalogue record for this book is available from the British Library

Notice

Clinical practice and medical knowledge constantly evolve. Standard safety precautions must be followed, but, as knowledge is broadened by research, changes in practice, treatment and drug therapy may become necessary or appropriate. Readers must check the most current product information provided by the manufacturer of each drug to be administered and verify the dosages and correct administration, as well as contraindications. It is the responsibility of the practitioner, utilising the experience and knowledge of the patient, to determine dosages and the best treatment for each individual patient. Any brands mentioned in this book are as examples only and are not endorsed by the publisher. Neither the publisher nor the authors assume any liability for any injury and/or damage to persons or property arising from this publication.

To contact M&K Publishing write to:

M&K Update Ltd · The Old Bakery · St. John's Street

Keswick · Cumbria CA12 5AS

Tel: 01768 773030 · Fax: 01768 781099

publishing@mkupdate.co.uk

www.mkupdate.co.uk

THE COMET LIBRARY
CLASS No. WB 354 BRo
ACC. No. 13729
DATE 10/2016
SUPPLIER Toms
COST £40.00

Designed and typeset by Mary Blood

Printed in Great Britain by Bell & Bain, Glasgow

The COMET Library
Luton & Dunstable Hospital
NHS Trust, Lewsey Road
LUTON LU4 0DZ

Tel: 01582 497201
E-mail: library@ldh.nhs.uk

Venepuncture and Cannulation
A practical guide

DATE DUE

		PRINTED IN U.S.A.

Other books from M&K include:

Clinical Examination Skills for Healthcare Professionals
ISBN: 9781905539710

Routine Blood Results Explained 3/e
ISBN: 9781905539888

Blood Results Explained in Clinical Practice
ISBN: 9781905539734

The ECG Workbook 2/e
ISBN: 9781905539772

Contents

Preface vii

About the author ix

Acknowledgements xi

1 What are venepuncture and cannulation? 1

2 An overview of the circulatory system and the related anatomy and physiology of the peripheral vascular system 5

3 Vein selection 13

4 Preparing yourself, your environment and your patient 23

5 Venepuncture techniques 27

6 Venepuncture – when things go wrong 43

7 Cannulation 49

8 Cannulation technique 57

9 Cannulation – when things go wrong 67

10 Reducing risks when carrying out venepuncture and cannulation 75

Appendix 1: Self-assessment checklist for venepuncture to ensure safe practice 83

Appendix 2: Self-assessment checklist for cannulation to ensure safe practice 85

References 87

Further reading 88

Index 89

Preface

Venepuncture and Cannulation: A practical guide offers an easy-to-read, comprehensive account of the practical procedures of venepuncture and intravenous cannulation. It provides the underlying theory and underpinning knowledge required as well as a step-by-step approach that will enable healthcare practitioners to master these vital skills.

This book is intended as a supplementary resource for individuals involved in practising or teaching these procedures, for healthcare practitioners wishing to update their knowledge, and for novice practitioners learning these skills for the first time.

Venepuncture and Cannulation: A practical guide is split into short chapters for ease of use. The reader can pick up and read relevant chapters according to their individual learning needs. Each chapter contains intended learning outcomes and points for practice. Some chapters also include activities to direct learning and considerations for practice. Chapter 1 defines venepuncture and cannulation, and explains why these procedures need to be undertaken. Chapter 2 gives a brief overview of the circulatory system, and identifies the relevant anatomy and physiology of the peripheral vascular system. Chapter 3 builds on Chapter 2, by considering the practicalities of choosing and assessing a vein, to ensure the success of each procedure. Chapter 4 discusses preparing the practitioner, the environment and the patient, which are fundamental aspects of venepuncture and cannulation procedures. Chapter 5 focuses on venepuncture techniques, from choosing a device to the equipment needed and the care of the venepuncture site.

Of course, things sometimes go wrong, so Chapter 6 looks at the potential complications of venepuncture and how to put things right. Chapter 7 focuses on the skill of cannulation, and cannula selection, care and the equipment needed. Chapter 8 then demonstrates the correct cannulation technique. Chapter 9 looks specifically at complications that occur in relation to cannulation, and includes guidance on how to put things right. Finally, consideration of risk is central to the success of both procedures. Accordingly, Chapter 10 focuses on risk, infection control, health and safety, and ethical and professional issues.

About the author

Nicola Brooks is a Senior Lecturer in Adult Nursing at De Montfort University. She is the Pre-Registration Lead for the undergraduate BSc (Hons) nursing programme. Her clinical background is practice education and surgical nursing, focusing on upper and lower gastro-intestinal surgery.

Acknowledgements

This book is dedicated to my beloved dad, who provided emotional, practical and, probably most importantly, financial support throughout my early nursing career.

Many thanks to **Cormac Norton**, Deputy Programme Leader and Senior Lecturer in Emergency Care at De Montfort University, who has written Chapter 2 and contributed to Chapter 3 of this book. Cormac's clinical background is in emergency medicine and nurse prescribing.

I would also like to extend my eternal gratitude to my mum for the endless offers of childcare to enable me to get this book written! From the bottom of my heart, I love you always.

Lastly, I would like to thank my partner, Paul Massarella, for keeping me fed and watered whilst I spent days at (his) laptop, my family and amazing friends for not only believing in me, but for giving me motivation, laughter and energy to get through when it looked as if it was never going to end… To my 'spa girls', especially, this is for you!

Nicola Brooks

Chapter 1

What are venepuncture and cannulation?

Learning outcomes

At the end of this chapter, the practitioner will be able to:

- Identify what the terms venepuncture and cannulation mean
- Identify reasons why venepuncture and/or cannulation may be needed.

Defining venepuncture and cannulation

Venepuncture is described as 'entering a needle into a vein' (Dougherty & Lister 2011) to obtain a blood sample for laboratory analysis (Lavery & Ingram 2005). Intravenous (IV) cannulation is a procedure whereby a plastic tube is temporarily inserted into a peripheral vein in order to gain access to the circulatory system (Scales 2005).

Both these procedures used to be exclusively performed by medical staff, with up to 80% of hospitalised patients receiving a cannula for intravenous therapy at some point during their stay (Dougherty & Lister 2011, Dougherty 2000). With an increasing number of patients being treated for acute and chronic illnesses, venepuncture and cannulation have become two of the most common everyday procedures in healthcare. It is also now widely accepted that these procedures may be carried out by all healthcare professionals, including unregistered practitioners, as part of their extended role.

Individuals wanting to undertake either of these procedures must undergo a period of training and supervision before they can perform them on patients. It is recognised that carrying out venepuncture and IV cannulation not only requires technical skill; it also requires specialist knowledge, good communication skills, time and patience (Davies 1998, Dougherty & Lamb 2008). These procedures can potentially cause pain and distress to patients, especially if the person performing them is not competent.

According to the Standards for Infusion Therapy (RCN 2010), practitioners must undergo theoretical and practical training in the following aspects in order to gain competency in the insertion of an IV cannula:

- Anatomy and physiology, particularly the anatomy of the veins, arteries, nerves and underlying tissue structures
- Patient assessment and patient's perspective
- Improving venous access (for example, through pharmacological and non-pharmacological methods)
- Selection of veins and problems associated with venous access; prevention and management of complications
- Selection of device and equipment
- Risk management
- Performing the procedure
- Monitoring and care of the site
- Documentation.

Once assessed as competent by a suitably qualified practitioner, it is essential that an individual maintains their level of competence, and that they get ongoing practice in the procedure. The Nursing and Midwifery Council (2010) state in the NMC Code that 'to practise competently, you must possess the knowledge, skills and abilities required for lawful, safe and effective practice without direct supervision'. This is echoed for allied health professionals by the Health and Care Professionals Council (2008) who say in their 'Standards of conduct, performance and ethics' that an individual must 'act within the limits of knowledge, skills and experience and, if necessary, refer the matter to another professional'. It is accepted that venepuncture and IV cannulation may also be performed by unregistered practitioners. Although these staff members are not currently registered by a professional body, it is worth checking your local healthcare provider's policy, procedure or guidelines to check that they are covered to perform these procedures. This will ensure unregistered practitioners' protection and safety.

Why do we need to perform venepuncture?

Venepuncture is usually requested to assist in diagnosis, to monitor a patient's condition, or to determine the effectiveness of a particular medical treatment. Blood analysis is one of the most commonly used and important diagnostic tools available to clinicians. We rely on blood results to help us interpret many clinical signs and symptoms. Developing an accurate venepuncture technique can therefore help facilitate holistic and timely treatment for patients.

A sample of circulating blood is taken to the laboratory for one of the following:

- Haematological blood analysis
- Biochemical blood analysis
- Bacteriological blood analysis.

Reflection

Think about the specific blood tests that are undertaken within your practice area. What are the usual reasons for blood sampling and the common tests and investigations that are carried out?

Chapter 5 provides a detailed explanation of venepuncture technique and describes the correct procedure for taking blood samples. Detailed explanations of the different blood tests taken (and the reasons for them) can be found in other publications, particularly the titles listed under Further Reading on p. 88, such as *Routine Blood Results Explained* (Bland 2008) or *Blood Results in Clinical Practice* (Basten 2013), which are simple texts that are easy to read and understand.

Why do we need to perform cannulation?

There are many different reasons why a patient may require insertion of an IV cannula. These may include:

- Administration of IV fluids to maintain hydration and/or to correct dehydration in those patients who are unable to tolerate sufficient oral fluid
- Administration of IV medication (either bolus, intermittent or a continuous infusion)

- Transfusion of blood or blood products
- Provision of IV access for nutritional support
- Assistance in close observation and monitoring of a patient.

A cannula is also sometimes inserted 'just in case'. This may not usually be an accepted rationale for cannulation. However, an IV cannula is often inserted into a vein for particular patients whose condition could quickly deteriorate. In such a situation, a fast response would be required and having a cannula already in place could save vital minutes (for instance, for those at risk of major haemorrhage).

The decision to insert an IV cannula will usually be made by medical staff or by a suitably qualified healthcare professional. In some practice settings, the decision may form part of a care pathway or protocol.

Summary

Always ensure that the decision to insert an IV cannula is based on professional knowledge and judgement. You must also take care to follow your local healthcare provider's policy, procedure or guidelines for undertaking IV cannulation.

Chapter 2

An overview of the circulatory system and the related anatomy and physiology of the peripheral vascular system

Cormac Norton

Learning outcomes

At the end of this chapter, the practitioner will be able to:

- Understand the structure of the circulatory system
- Identify the structural differences between an artery and a vein
- Distinguish between an artery and a vein
- Understand the basic anatomy and physiology of the peripheral vascular system.

Understanding the structure of the circulatory system

The human circulatory system has three key components:

- Heart
- Blood
- Blood vessels.

Heart

The heart is a four-chambered pump. The pumping action of the heart can appear confusing. It may therefore help to separate functions that occur on the right side of the heart from functions that occur on the left.

Table 2.1: Right-side heart functions

- Deoxygenated blood is delivered to the *right atrium* by two of the largest veins in the body – the inferior and superior venae cavae.
- The *right atrium* pumps blood to the *right ventricle*.
- The *right ventricle* pumps blood to the lungs for oxygenation via the *pulmonary artery*.

The right side of the heart contains two of the heart's four chambers – the right atrium and the right ventricle. The primary role of the right side is to pump deoxygenated blood to the lungs (Peate & Nair 2011). Deoxygenated blood enters the right side of the heart. From there, it travels to the lungs.

At this point it is useful to highlight one of the key differences between arteries and veins:

Arteries carry blood away from the heart; veins carry blood back to the heart.

The venae cavae (large veins) therefore carry blood *back* to the heart, while the pulmonary artery carries blood *away* from the heart. Once the blood has been oxygenated, it travels from the lungs to the left side of the heart and, from there, on to the rest of the body.

Table 2.2: Left-side heart functions

- Once blood has been oxygenated in the lungs it is carried back to the *left atrium* via the *pulmonary vein*.
- The *left atrium* pumps blood into the *left ventricle*.
- The *left ventricle* is the most powerful chamber of the heart and pumps blood via the *aorta* (the largest artery in the body).
- The *aorta* carries blood to the rest of body through a network of arteries (Peate & Nair 2011).

Blood

Blood is essential for life and has several functions within the human body. Its three key functions are listed below:

1 Transport: Blood carries oxygen, glucose, electrolytes and other nutrients to cells to enable those cells to function. Waste products from the cells are carried away by the blood for elimination. These waste products include carbon dioxide, for example.

2 Defence: Cells in the blood play a vital role in the body's immune system. These 'defensive cells' include white cells and antibodies. The blood can also coagulate, forming clots and scabs. This helps prevent further injury to the body from fluid loss.

3 Maintenance of homeostasis: This is a process by which the blood helps to control body temperature and the pH (acid and alkali balance) within the body.

Blood vessels

There are five types of blood vessel:

- Arteries
- Arterioles
- Capillaries
- Venules
- Veins.

Blood first travels away from the heart via the aorta (an artery). Gradually, as the blood travels through the network of arteries, the arteries become narrower, and eventually they become arterioles. These arterioles enter tissue and continue to branch out and reduce in size as they do so.

The arterioles then branch into tiny vessels called capillaries. At this point, the exchange of materials occurs. For example, oxygen will leave the blood and enter the cell, and waste products will leave the cells and enter the blood (Peate & Nair 2011).

The blood now begins its journey back to the heart. As the capillaries leave the tissue they become venules. As the vessels continue they increase in size becoming veins. Finally all the veins converge into the vena cava returning the blood to the right side of the heart (Peate & Nair 2011).

Understanding the structural differences between an artery and a vein

Apart from the functional differences between an artery and a vein discussed above, there are some structural differences that are important in relation to venepuncture and intravenous cannulation.

Both arteries and veins consist of three layers of tissue:

1. The outermost layer: the Tunica Externa, which gives support and stability
2. The middle layer: the Tunica Media, which allows for changing blood flow and pressure
3. The innermost layer: the Tunica Intima, which facilitates blood flow.

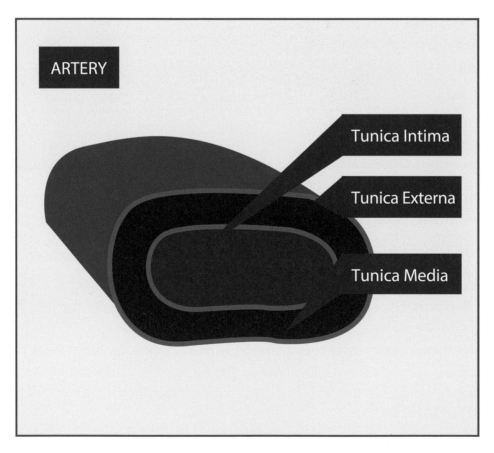

Figure 2.1: The structure of the artery

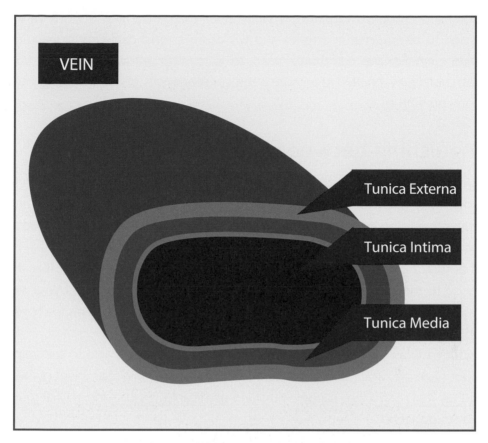

Figure 2.2: The structure of the vein

Arteries are designed to carry blood travelling at relatively high pressure (such as 120mmHg). Veins carry blood at a much lower pressure – for example, around 80mmHg.

The key structural difference between an artery and a vein is the Tunica Media. In arteries this middle layer consists of thick, elastic, muscular tissue, which enables the artery to expand and respond quickly to a rise in pressure. This elasticity allows arteries to propel the blood as it travels from the heart (Tortora & Derrickson 2011).

When carrying out venepuncture for blood sampling, it is important not to inadvertently puncture an artery with the needle or the cannula. Penetration of an artery can lead to a large and fast-filling haematoma (a localised collection of blood outside the blood vessel, within the tissue), which can cause significant discomfort and complications for the person undergoing the procedure.

In terms of cannulation, this text relates *only* to intravenous cannulation. When performing cannulation, it is crucial to cannulate a vein rather than an artery. Venous cannulas are not designed to be inserted in arteries and will cause arterial damage. More importantly, intravenous cannulas are commonly used to administer intravenous drugs. Should a cannula be mistakenly inserted in an artery, the consequences of administering intravenous medication could be fatal.

Distinguishing between veins and arteries

To distinguish between veins and arteries, feel for the radial artery in your wrist on the palm side of your hand (about 5cm below the base of your thumb). If you roll your index and middle fingers over the artery, you will feel a round, yet elastic 'tube'. You will also feel the pulsations through the artery. This pulsation is caused by the artery expanding in response to blood pumped by the left ventricle. The artery then contracts, ensuring that the blood can continue to the hand. If you move your fingers towards the centre of your wrist, you will feel a very rigid structure travelling from your elbow to your hand. This is a tendon. This feels solid, does not pulsate and moves when you move your fingers.

Turn your hand around and hang it by your side. You should be able to see veins on the back of your hand become more prominent. Gently feel the most prominent of these veins. Although they feel round they cannot withstand significant pressure and go 'flat' quite easily. A vein has no pulsation.

Veins, unlike arteries, do not have a robust, muscular middle layer. In contrast, the Tunica Externa is much thicker than the equivalent layer in an artery. This allows veins to expand, but unlike arteries they are not elastic, and therefore cannot pulsate in the same manner as an artery. When blood pressure is reduced it may still be possible to be able to feel (palpate) arteries. However, veins appear to collapse and may be impossible to palpate.

One further structural difference, which is relevant to venepuncture and cannulation, is that veins have valves, whereas arteries do not. These valves ensure that blood flows in one direction, to assist with venous return. As you will read later in Chapters 7 and 10, it is not unusual for practitioners to have problems with cannulating or when performing venepuncture due to a valve occluding (blocking) the lumen (channel) of the cannula or needle.

Understanding the related anatomy of the peripheral vascular system

For the purpose of this chapter, it is assumed that the practitioner will be undertaking uncomplicated venepuncture or cannulation in the upper limbs. Central venous access or complicated venepuncture carries additional hazards and requires specialist skills that are not covered in this text. Although not functionally relevant to venepuncture or cannulation, the bones serve as useful landmarks when identifying sites at which to perform these procedures. In the forearm, the radius extends from the elbow to just below the thumb. It can be palpated at the prominence known as the radial styloid, just proximal to the thumb. The radius can be palpated towards the elbow until it is barely palpable below the brachioradialis muscle in the forearm to its origin at the radial head as part of the elbow. This bone lends its name to both the radial artery and the radial nerve. It therefore serves as a useful landmark. To find the radial pulse, one simply needs to palpate for the pulse on the palmar side of the radial styloid.

Likewise, the ulna can be palpated very easily and lends its name to both the ulnar artery and nerve. The ulnar nerve can be palpated on the palmar side of the ulnar styloid, and the ulnar nerve lies very close to this structure.

The elbow consists of three bones – the radius, the ulna and the humerus. The radius and ulna form the lower arm; and the humerus forms the upper arm. If the arm is held with the palm of the hand facing forwards (facing the ceiling), the anterior surface of the elbow (the area facing uppermost), when relaxed, forms a natural dip. This is known as the antecubital fossa, and it is a very common site for venepuncture and cannulation.

It is essential for practitioners to be able to identify the major arterial branches within the upper limb and locate the principal sites at which to perform venepuncture and cannulation. Nerves and arteries are commonly found directly adjacent to each other, forming a neurovascular bundle. The practitioner must ensure that they avoid both structures when attempting venepuncture and cannulation.

Activity

Firstly, try to identify the major vein branches in your arm. This will help you decide which vein to choose for either venepuncture or cannulation. You can always compare your veins with those of a colleague. However, every individual is unique and will have veins that may look and feel slightly different from someone else's. Secondly, try to identify the major arterial branches of the upper limb:

- **The brachial artery**

- **The radial artery**
- **The ulnar artery.**

This will give you an indication of places to avoid when choosing a site for venepuncture or cannulation.

Summary

An awareness of anatomy and physiology is essential before undertaking either cannulation or venepuncture. You need to have an adequate knowledge of the circulatory system and of the structures of veins and arteries, tendons and nerves before attempting these procedures. This chapter only provides a basic insight into these subjects so you may need to explore them in more detail, using a dedicated anatomy and physiology book such as Peate & Nair (2011).

Chapter 3

Vein selection

Learning outcomes

At the end of this chapter, the practitioner will be able to:

- Identify common sites for venepuncture and cannulation
- Determine the criteria for choosing a vein
- Consider the factors that may determine vein choice
- Get 'top tips' on how to make veins more prominent.

It is essential that healthcare practitioners know about the anatomy and physiology of the arteries, veins, nerves and bone structure so that the most appropriate site can be chosen for venepuncture or cannulation (see Chapter 2 for a brief overview of the anatomy and physiology of the peripheral vascular system). It is worth taking some time before undertaking either procedure to assess the patient's veins. Choosing the most suitable and healthy vein may determine the success (or otherwise) of the procedure, as well as ensuring that it is as safe, appropriate and pain-free as possible.

Identifying common sites for venepuncture and cannulation

The superficial veins of the upper limb are most commonly used for both venepuncture and cannulation because they are located just beneath the skin (Richardson 2008). These are called the cephalic or basilic veins. The median cubital vein, located within the antecubital fossa, is ideal for venepuncture because it is easily located, well supported and easy to palpate (Ernst 2005). This vein is often referred to as 'the phlebotomist's friend' and it is the first choice for venepuncture. (A phlebotomist is an unregistered professional, whose role is to perform venepuncture.) This site is not always suitable for cannulation though, because of location of the joints, which may ultimately increase the risk of thromboembolism – the formation of a clot in the blood that blocks a blood vessel (Scales 2005).

If you are unable to find a suitable vein in the upper limb, the metacarpal veins (in the hand) could be considered. If no alternative sites are available in either the upper limbs or the hands, it may be necessary to refer the procedure on to medical staff. In practice, you may have seen medics perform the procedure using veins in the patient's feet – the dorsum of the foot or the saphenous vein of the ankle. For healthcare professionals, and particularly nursing staff, the Royal College of Nursing (2010) *do not* advocate the routine use of these sites due to the risk of complications, specifically thrombophlebitis and pulmonary embolism (Weinstein 2007). For these reasons, many local healthcare providers will not allow the use of veins in the feet or ankles.

When selecting a vein, it is important to remember that there may be some variation in vein position between individuals. Arteries are usually positioned deeply, but some individuals may have an artery located superficially in an unusual place. This is known as an aberrant artery.

Table 3.1: Veins of choice

- Cephalic vein
- Basilic vein
- Median cubital vein
- Metacarpal veins (veins of the hand).

Cephalic vein

The cephalic vein extends from the dorsal veins in the hand and goes upwards on the outer lateral aspect of the arm (the radial side of the arm). The cephalic vein is naturally very large and this makes it an excellent vessel for cannulation, as its position provides a natural splint. However, care needs to be taken as the cephalic vein, which lies near the wrist, can also lie very close to the radial nerve.

The cephalic vein can be most easily found on the radial border of the wrist. This vein can be easily accessed, but is not always suitable for cannulation due to its proximity to the radial styloid. This can make movement of the wrist uncomfortable with a cannula in place.

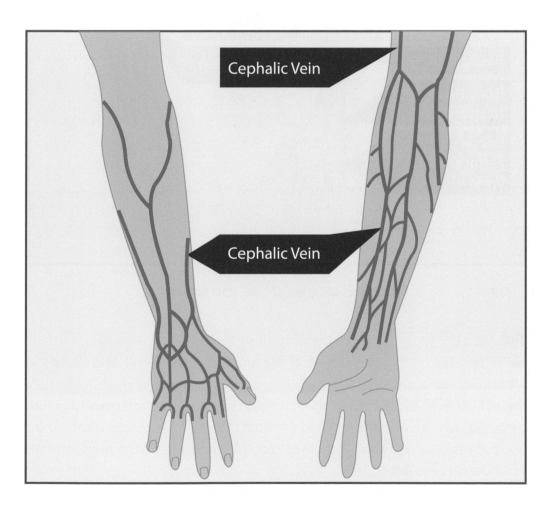

Figure 3.1: Location of the cephalic vein

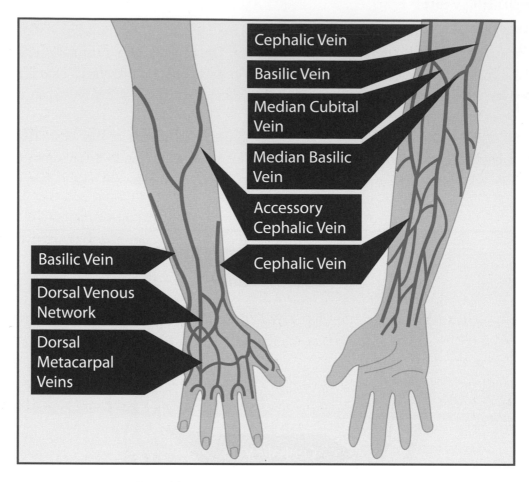

Figure 3.2: Location of the superficial veins

Basilic vein

The basilic vein lies on the inner aspect of the arm and starts at the ulnar border of the hand. The basilic vein is similar to the cephalic, in so far as it is a large vessel that appears prominent. However, it is often overlooked for both venepuncture and cannulation because it tends to 'roll', which makes the procedure difficult (McCall & Tankersley 2008). The basilic vein also has many valves (which help keep blood flowing toward the heart) and this can make cannulation problematic.

Median cubital vein

To locate the median cubital vein, turn the palm of the hand forward, facing uppermost, and allow a very slight bend in the elbow. The antecubital fossa is the natural hollow formed in front of the elbow joint. This site is very commonly used for venepuncture and intravenous cannulation due to the prominence of easily accessible, large, superficial veins.

As previously mentioned, the antecubital fossa is the most common venepuncture site – with the median cubital being the vein that is most commonly selected (Tortora & Derrickson 2011). Remember that the exact location of arteries and veins varies from person to person.

Although the arteries and nerves lie much deeper than the veins used for venepuncture, practitioners should be aware of their presence. The location of the brachial artery can be located by palpation in the antecubital fossa, and will be felt as a pulsation. The radial nerve travels close to the brachial artery but lies quite deep. Care should be taken to avoid both structures during venepuncture.

Metacarpal veins (veins of the hand)

The metacarpal veins on the hand can be considered for both venepuncture and short-term intravenous cannulation, as they are often easily visualised and palpated. The metacarpal bones of the hand provide the practitioner with a natural splint, which can help to secure a device (Scales 2008). The disadvantage is that these veins are often smaller in diameter than those in the forearm, tend to 'roll' easily, and may be difficult to stabilise at times. This is a particular problem with elderly or frail patients.

Dorsal venous network of the foot (veins of the foot)

As mentioned earlier, there are also veins in the lower extremities, located on the dorsum of the foot, and the saphenous vein in the ankle. These veins are similar to veins in the hand, in that they are smaller in diameter, and can easily 'roll'. Using these veins for cannulation is poor practice, and should almost always be avoided due to the increased risk of thrombophlebitis (Weinstein 2007). If a cannula is positioned in the lower extremity, it should be re-sited as soon as a more suitable vein is available (Dougherty 2008). Your local healthcare provider's policy or guidelines will almost certainly not support this practice by healthcare practitioners so approval and consent by medical staff should always be sought on the very rare occasions on which this site has to be used.

Table 3.2: Summary of vein choice

Vein	Advantages	Disadvantages
Cephalic vein	• Ideal vein choice for cannulation • Large vessel, excellent for administration of Intravenous (IV) therapies • Position in the forearm provides a natural splint	• May be uncomfortable for the patient due to position at the joint • Close to the radial nerve
Median cubital vein	• Ideal vein choice for venepuncture • Easily visualised, located and palpated • Known as the phlebotomist's friend	• Not suitable for cannulation due to the inability to flex and extend the arm
Basilic vein	• Large vessel	• Has many valves, which can make cannulation difficult • Vein can 'roll' easily
Metacarpal veins (veins of the hand)	• Suitable for venepuncture and short-term cannulation • Position on the back of the hand provides a natural splint • Easily accessible and palpated • Can consider using a winged infusion device for venepuncture if it is likely to be a difficult procedure	• Veins tend to be smaller Can 'roll' easily, particularly in elderly patients • Can be painful for the patient

Identifying venepuncture and cannulation sites in children

This text focuses on venepuncture and cannulation for the adult patient only. Competent and experienced practitioners should perform venepuncture or intravenous cannulation on children and neonates, as the procedure will require patience from the practitioner's perspective, and a detailed knowledge and understanding of child development. The choice of veins in a child may vary from using scalp veins or the feet (for infants and toddlers), to hand and arm veins (for toddlers to adolescents). If complications do occur, they can be much more serious than those in an adult.

Determining the criteria for choosing a suitable vein

When thinking about the most suitable vein to choose, the most important factor to consider is what will be best for the patient. So ask them! Your patient will be able to let you know which site (if any) has been used before, which was the easiest and also if there were any problems with a previous procedure. This is really important when considering intravenous cannulation, as the device can be intrusive, uncomfortable and potentially impair limb extension and flexion. As you have seen from the vein choice summary in Table 3.2 above, the most prominent vein may not always be the most suitable.

There are two stages when locating a suitable vein:

1. Visual inspection
2. Palpation.

1. Visual inspection

Visual inspection allows you to look at the location of the vein and assess whether it is suitable to use. You should avoid areas that show signs of infection – for example, if they are damaged or bruised, swollen or have been used repeatedly for either venepuncture or cannulation. You should *always* carry out a visual inspection before applying a tourniquet.

2. Palpation

Palpation should occur after visual inspection, as it enables you to feel the location, size and condition of the vein. With clean hands, palpate the vein using the tip of the index finger. You should run your finger over the vein, gently pressing down to feel the structure of the vein wall. Palpation will help you to ensure that you select the most suitable blood vessel. Practice makes perfect with palpating veins, and it is a skill that is acquired.

NB: Do not use your thumb to palpate a vein, as it is not as sensitive as your fingers. The thumb also has a pulse, which may cause confusion.

Activity

Practise visual inspection and palpation on a colleague's vein. What does the vein look like and how does it feel?

Considering the factors that may determine vein choice

There are many different reasons why some veins may not be used or will be unsuitable for venepuncture or intravenous cannulation. For example, disease, injury or illness may prevent use. Always ask the patient, and seek medical advice from an experienced colleague, where possible, if you are unsure whether your vein choice may be contraindicated.

Cerebral Vascular Accident (CVA)

Venepuncture or cannulation is contraindicated on a limb affected by CVA, as the patient may have little or no sensation. This in turn could prevent the patient from detecting any pain during or after the procedure (Dougherty 2008). In addition, restricted movement may prevent the patient from moving the limb to a comfortable position in which to undertake the procedure.

Scars from burns or surgery

Any area that is scarred from a burn or surgery should be avoided, as the vein may be difficult to palpate, and the skin hard to puncture. Healed burn sites may also have impaired circulation, and this can potentially lead to inaccurate blood results. The practitioner should avoid areas that have had recent tattoos, as there may be a risk of infection if the skin is broken and the area is still healing. Another consideration is that dyes used in tattoos may potentially lead to inaccurate blood results (McCall & Tankersley 2008).

Oedematous areas

Swelling can make palpation of the vein difficult, and applying a tourniquet may in turn cause further tissue damage. Accessing oedematous limbs may lead to contamination of the sample with fluid. Fluid accumulation is known to alter blood test results.

Surgery or treatment in the axillary area

Venepuncture or cannulation should be avoided if the patient has had previous surgery or treatment to the axillary area. This commonly affects patients who have had breast surgery for cancer (such as a mastectomy), or those patients with lymphoedema. Application of a tourniquet may predispose the patient to further injury and/or infection if the affected limb is used for the procedure. If a patient has had bilateral treatment, refer to your local healthcare provider's policy or seek medical advice.

Intravenous infusion (IVI)

If the patient has an intravenous (IVI) infusion running, then you should not use the arm for venepuncture. Any samples taken above the IV site may be contaminated with the solution, and infused products may dilute or elevate the results taken from your specimen (Ernst 2005). Always refer to your local healthcare provider's policy if another site cannot be used. Many local healthcare providers have a protocol in place specifying that the infusion can be switched off for a period of time to allow venous blood samples to be taken. If you are unsure, seek medical advice.

Other considerations when judging the suitability of veins

These may include:

- Recent venepuncture or cannulation sites: repeatedly using the same site can cause damage and thrombosis (hardening) of the affected vein
- Patient position: consider how your patient is positioned; for instance, are they mobile or confined to a bed/chair?
- Temperature of the environment: if it is too hot or too cold, vasodilation (widening of the blood vessel) or vasoconstriction (narrowing of the blood vessel) may occur.
- Anxiety: if the patient is anxious, vasoconstriction may occur, which can make visual inspection and palpation difficult. Adequate patient preparation is vital to overcome this problem; this is discussed in detail in Chapter 4.

Table 3.3: Visual inspection and palpation checklist

When visually inspecting and palpating veins:

- Choose a vein that has not been used recently
- Select a vein that is easily inspected and palpated (feels soft and bouncy to the touch)
- Choose a vein that is well supported
- Ask your patient if they can recommend veins to be selected or avoided
- Consider your patient's comfort
- *Avoid* hard, fragile, mobile or thrombosed veins, or those that lie over bony prominences.

Top tips for making veins more prominent

If you are struggling to visually inspect and palpate a suitable vein, there are numerous ways to help make the vein more prominent. The 'top tips' listed below may be helpful.

1. Applying a tourniquet

This helps to promote venous return and venous distention. However, take care not to apply the tourniquet too tightly, as this may restrict blood flow and cause damage to arteries and veins. As a rule of thumb, you should apply your tourniquet about 7–8cm above the site (Witt 2008). Do not place it too tight – you should always be able to place your finger between the tourniquet and the patient's limb. Do not keep the tourniquet tightened on the limb for any longer than a minute. If you are considering using a tourniquet, then refer to your local healthcare provider's policy first to ensure that your practice is correct. Many local healthcare providers advocate using a disposable ('single use') tourniquet, to reduce the risk of transmitting infection between patients.

2. Use gravity

Lowering the arm below the level of the heart helps to promote venous distention, and increases the blood supply to the veins. This may help the vein look more prominent (become more engorged with blood).

3. Warm the limb

Warming the limb increases venous distention and helps improve the 'filling' of the vein. The limb can be warmed either by using a heat pack or by immersing it in warm (not hot) water.

4 Stimulate the vein

You can lightly stroke the vein to promote vasodilation. Tapping the vein is not advised, as it can be painful for the patient and cause bruising.

5 Clench the fist

Ask the patient to gently open and close the fist. This action helps the muscles to force blood into veins and promotes venous distention.

Summary

In this chapter we have considered the most common sites for venepuncture and cannulation. Specifically, ideas and a rationale for appropriate vein selection have been considered, as well as some contraindications for vein choice. By taking time to select the most appropriate vein, the practitioner will increase the chances of carrying out a successful procedure first time. Chapter 5 discusses the equipment required, and focuses on the venepuncture technique. Chapters 8 and 9 both focus on the skill of cannulation.

Chapter 4

Preparing yourself, your environment and your patient

Learning outcomes

At the end of this chapter, the practitioner will be able to:

- Correctly prepare yourself and your environment
- Adequately prepare the patient for the procedure.

In order to perform a successful venepuncture or cannulation technique, it is vitally important that you prepare yourself, your environment and your patient correctly.

Preparing yourself and your environment

Ensure that you have all the correct equipment ready (see Chapter 5 for the specific equipment needed for venepuncture, and Chapter 8 if you are performing cannulation). This includes a pair of well-fitting gloves to protect you from blood spillage or contamination (Perruca 2001). Recent EU directives (2013) state that the wearing of gloves is a minimum requirement. An apron and goggles will further reduce the risk of contamination through blood splashing.

In clinical practice you may see practitioners or medical staff performing these procedures without gloves. However, this is bad practice and it is important that you adopt the correct techniques when learning these skills in order to protect yourself and your patient. The risks of latex allergies are well known, so consider the types of gloves that you have available to minimise the risk of exposure to harmful substances (MDA 1996) to both you and your patient. You may also want to consider wearing a disposable apron, again, in case of blood spillage.

Points for your practice

When using a tourniquet, make sure that it is cleaned between each patient use. Or, alternatively, use a 'single-use' disposable tourniquet. Refer to your local healthcare provider's policy to ensure that you are following the correct practice.

There should be adequate lighting of the environment to ensure that you can perform an accurate venous assessment. The room should be warm to encourage vasodilation (widening of the blood vessels). If the room is too cold, vasoconstriction (narrowing of the blood vessels) may occur, thus making the procedure more difficult. If you are finding it difficult to make an accurate venous assessment, you may wish to use some of the methods listed in Chapter 3 (see p. 22) to encourage vasodilation.

You also need to make sure that you are in a comfortable position. Consider whether you need to raise or lower the height of the bed or chair to avoid unnecessary bending or twisting. Ensure that you are generally comfortable and relaxed. This is particularly important when you are new to performing either procedure, as gaining confidence and competence takes time. Use an experienced colleague to support you through the procedure if necessary – particularly if it may be a challenging situation, or the patient is anxious.

Preparing the patient

There are many considerations when preparing your patient for venepuncture or intravenous cannulation. Firstly, make sure that you explain everything to them. If your patient understands what is going to be done, they are more likely to co-operate. This will save you time, but – more importantly – it will benefit the patient, as it may help alleviate their fears, and to some extent will reduce any pain associated with the procedure. Anxiety can be easily triggered, perhaps due to a previous bad experience, a needle phobia or a general dislike of needles (Lavery & Ingram 2005). Providing clear and comprehensive information about the procedure and aftercare will help to reduce the patient's level of anxiety.

You may also want to consider the use of pharmacological interventions (such as applying a local anaesthetic cream or gel to the area – for example, EMLA cream). Pharmacological interventions can be particularly beneficial for children, when inserting larger-gauge cannulae, or simply if the patient requests them (Dougherty & Watson 2011). These interventions are often under-used in clinical practice. You could also consider other forms of distraction – for example, music therapy. Wendler (2003) mentions that coughing at the moment of insertion distracts the patient and reduces pain. Once you have reassured and explained everything in detail, you can gain the patient's consent.

Points for your practice

Ernst & Ernst (2001) listed their 'Four secrets to a painless procedure', which you may want to consider when preparing yourself, your environment and your patient:

1. Check vein choice: Use the median cubital vein (rather than the cephalic or basilic vein) for venepuncture, as this will cause less discomfort.

2. Check needle size/type: Use the smallest gauge cannula to make insertion into the vein easier.

3. Ensure that there is good anchoring of the skin by holding it down to avoid skin movement.

4. Ensure that the skin is dry: This prevents a burning sensation of alcohol when skin is punctured, and reduces the risk of the sample being contaminated.

It is important to gain the patient's consent prior to either procedure being performed. Consent is frequently implied by the patient's actions (such as holding out their arm). However, this has no legal standing, so it is better for consent to be given verbally by the patient. As Lavery (2003) points out, for consent to be valid it must be given voluntarily, without influence or pressure to accept treatment. Verbal consent is usually accepted with these procedures, though written consent may be required if either procedure forms part of a research study.

Once you have provided your patient with sufficient information and gained their consent, you need to consider their physical and mental well-being. Firstly, allow the patient some time to go to the toilet if they wish. They may also want to hold someone's hand before you start, to ensure that they are relaxed. Secondly, make sure that your patient is in a comfortable position, either on a bed or in a chair with their limb supported with pillows or a cushion. Placing the limb on a pillow or rolled-up towel gives the patient some support, as well as providing a firm and flat surface for you to use.

Remember to consider the patient's privacy and dignity at all times – for example, if you need to remove clothing in order to perform the procedure. If your patient is anxious or distressed, consider asking a colleague to help support them. A smiling face or some relaxing and soothing words before, during and after the procedure may help reduce the patient's level of anxiety. Once you have completed the procedure, it is equally important to leave the patient comfortable, as well as providing an opportunity for them to ask questions about any aftercare that may be needed.

Reflection

Have you had blood taken or a cannula inserted? How did this make you feel at the time? Did the person carrying out the procedure say or do anything that helped put you at ease?

Summary

In this chapter, we have considered the preparation of the practitioner, the environment and – most importantly – the patient. You will need to reflect on the content of this chapter before practising venepuncture or intravenous cannulation. Think about the environment in which you will be undertaking these procedures and consider any improvements that can be made in order to make the procedure more pleasant for yourself and your patient.

Chapter 5

Venepuncture techniques

Learning outcomes

At the end of this chapter, the practitioner will be able to:

- Select the appropriate device with which to perform venepuncture
- Identify the equipment needed to perform the procedure
- Follow an appropriate 'Order of draw' for obtaining a blood sample
- Have a detailed knowledge of the correct venepuncture technique, whether using a vacuum system or a 'winged device'
- Care for the puncture site correctly
- Apply the principles of venepuncture to everyday practice.

It is important to follow your local healthcare provider's policy when undertaking this procedure. Some policies are very detailed, and include step-by-step guidelines, as well as an explanation of why things are done in a particular way. They may also provide you with useful additional reading and a detailed understanding of the important processes to be considered when performing venepuncture.

Activity

Find and read your local healthcare provider's venepuncture policy and guidelines. Make sure that you understand and follow the working practices detailed in them before undertaking venepuncture.

Choosing a venepuncture device

The most common way of collecting blood is the vacuum system. This works by using plastic blood collection tubes that are sealed with rubber stoppers, creating a partial vacuum. The air pressure in the tube is negative. Inserting the blood collection bottle creates a difference in the pressure between the collection bottle and the vein, and this causes the tube to fill. The vacuum will cause the blood collection tube to fill to the required pre-set level and then stop. There are many types of vacuum systems available, designed by different manufacturers, so it is important to find out which one is used in your local area.

Alternatively, blood can be collected using a needle and syringe or winged infusion device ('butterfly'). There are certain winged infusion devices that are manufactured for blood collection sets. These are the best choice in cases where it may be difficult to obtain an adequate blood sample from a patient, due to poor vein quality or a needle phobia. This approach can be considered when taking samples from children. Hefler *et al.* (2004) found that using a winged infusion device was more successful in obtaining samples at the first attempt, particularly with older patients. Patients also reported less discomfort from blood collection taken from the median cubital vein, the forearm and the back of the hand. Before assembling the equipment you will need, you may wish to refer back to Chapter 3 ('Vein selection'), to remind yourself about the procedure for selecting an appropriate vein and identifying the vein of choice.

NB: Using a winged infusion device may not be supported by all local healthcare providers. Ensure that you check your local policy and guidelines before using this option.

Before you start the venepuncture procedure, you need to have the blood requisition (request) form completed, and know the blood tests that need to be taken. Check with your patient that any pre-test requirements (such as fasting, or having their medication administered at a specific time) have been adhered to. Do not begin unless you have all the required information prior to the procedure.

Activity

Look at the blood collection system most commonly used by your local healthcare provider. What is the choice available?

Identifying the equipment required for venepuncture

Use this checklist to ensure that you gather all the required equipment.

You will need a tray containing:

- A tourniquet, ideally 'single use' (disposable)
- Personal protective equipment (such as appropriately sized clean gloves and apron)
- Swabs to clean the insertion site, either alcohol-based or antiseptic, depending on your local healthcare provider's policy (70% isopropyl alcohol with 2% chlorhexidine is common practice and cleansing the skin reduces the risk of contamination)
- A blood collection set with appropriately sized needle gauge (the smallest gauge needle that is suitable for the vein and the sampling requirements); you will need an additional needle in case your first attempt is unsuccessful. A winged infusion device system can be used as an alternative for performing the procedure on smaller veins if required (check that the packaging is intact and has not expired prior to use; discard immediately if damaged or out of date).
- Appropriate requisition forms and blood specimen bags
- Blood specimen tubes required for testing
- Gauze and adhesive tape to cover the sampling site after the procedure
- A sharps bin and pillow should be close at hand.

There are a few general points to consider when taking blood samples for analysis:

1. Do not take blood from above the same vein that has an intravenous infusion in progress, as this will contaminate the results given and will provide an inaccurate reading, particularly when testing for electrolyte concentrations.
2. Too large a needle in a small vein can damage the vein (McCall & Tankersley 2008).

3. Using a needle that is too small may cause haemolysis (the rupture of red blood cells), leading to the release of their contents into the surrounding fluid). Needle sizes range from 20 to 23 gauge, and a 21-gauge needle is standard for most clinical situations (McCall & Tankersley 2008).

4. Prolonged application of a tourniquet can cause tissue damage and alter intracellular structure. Tissue damage can cause potassium to be released, thus providing inaccurate readings from the blood sample collected.

5. If test results appear altered or significantly abnormal, they should be repeated immediately if clinically indicated.

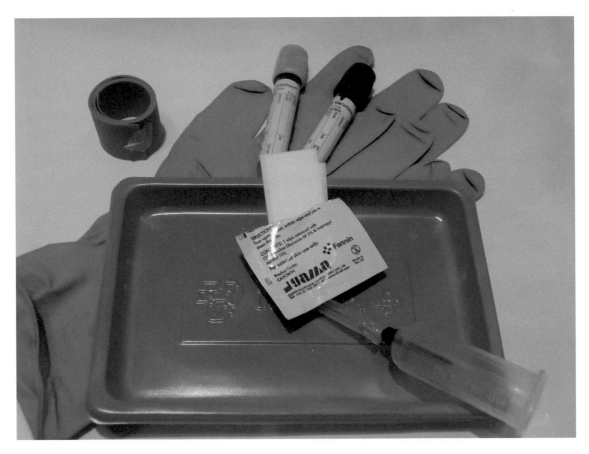

Figure 5.1: Blood collection vacuum system

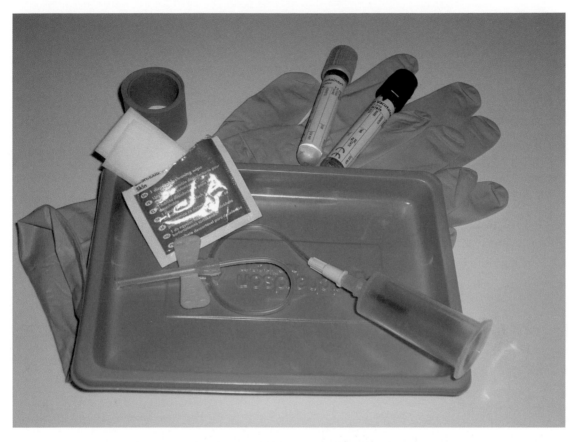

Figure 5.2: Blood collection winged infusion device

Following the appropriate 'order of draw'

When taking blood samples, it is important to take them in the right order. Samples must be taken in a specific order to avoid cross-contamination of additives between the tubes. Manufacturers standardise colours for the additives used in the blood collection tubes, although it is important to note that these colours may differ internationally. The manufacturers of blood tubes usually have coloured charts available that show the correct order of draw. It is advisable to display these prominently to prevent any mistakes.

Several different types of tubes are used in blood drawing. Each tube is identified by the color of the stopper and the additive placed in the tube. Each additive has a specific function.

As a general rule, blood samples should be taken in the following order:

1. Sterile tubes

2. Coagulation tubes

3. Serum tubes, heparin or plasma separator tubes

4. Ethylene diamine tetra acetic acid (EDTA) tubes

5. Glycolytic inhibitor or oxalate tubes.

It is vital that the correct order is followed in each and every blood draw. For example, if a sterile tube is drawn after another tube, you will forfeit the sterility and will risk contaminating that specimen. Likewise, if drawn out of order, EDTA can still be on the needle in trace amounts and may keep the next tube from clotting the way it is supposed to. Nor do you want to introduce heparin (a blood thinner) to a coagulation tube, since that would render your results inaccurate.

Identifying different tubes

- Sterile tubes are larger than the usual blood collection tubes.
- Coagulation tubes have stoppers that are light blue.
- Serum tubes can have a red stopper (with or without a clot activator in the bottom of the tube), a bright yellow plastic stopper or a red and grey speckled rubber top.
- Heparin and plasma separator tubes have light green or green and grey tops.
- EDTA is found in tubes with lavender stoppers.
- Grey-topped tubes are oxalate tubes or glycolytic inhibitors.

Any tubes with additives must be thoroughly mixed (or inverted) to avoid odd test results. Bottles must not be shaken. If in doubt, refer to the specific manufacturer's guidelines, which are available on the Internet. It is also useful to speak to biomedical scientists working in your local Trust laboratory if you are unsure. It is often well worth visiting the laboratory to see what happens to your samples after you take them – this will help you to understand the different processes that each blood sample goes through to get the final results.

Having gathered the necessary equipment, and prepared yourself, your environment and your patient, you need to develop an accurate venepuncture technique. This may look easy but, particularly when starting out, it can take time to master! You should have no more than two attempts at undertaking the procedure (Perruca 2001), using a different site each time, and make sure that you feel confident and competent to do this. If you are new to venepuncture, try to choose patients with 'good veins' whilst you are mastering the skill, as it is very easy to lose confidence if you are unsuccessful. If you are not able to obtain a blood sample after two attempts, or if it is a challenging situation in which to obtain samples, let a more experienced practitioner perform the procedure.

Following the correct venepuncture technique using a vacuum system

The key stages of the venepuncture technique using a vacuum system are listed in the table below.

Table 5.1: Correct venepuncture technique using a vacuum system

What to do	Why it is done
Always start by washing your hands with soap and water.	
1 Prepare the environment, thinking about the lighting and temperature.	To ensure that the practitioner is prepared to perform the procedure and that it can be carried out efficiently without interruption. This also ensures a safe working environment.
2 Gather all the equipment you will need, checking that the packaging is intact and none of the items has expired.	To ensure that the procedure is performed efficiently, safely and without distraction.
3 Identify the specific tests required on the requisition form and select the appropriate blood collection tubes and blood collection system.	To ensure that the correct samples are collected.
4 Identify the patient, checking their name band (where appropriate) or asking them to confirm their identity. Check these details against the blood requisition form. Check and confirm all details verbally with the patient.	To ensure that you have the correct patient.

5	Allow the patient time to ask any questions and provide information on how you will undertake the procedure.	To obtain the patient's consent and ensure their co-operation. Providing plenty of information will reduce their level of anxiety.
6	Determine the patient's preferred site for the procedure, based upon their previous experience, and ensure the patient's comfort once you have positioned them appropriately. For instance, they must be sitting comfortably and the arm must be supported (for example, using a pillow).	To maintain patient comfort, and to familiarise yourself with the patient's medical history and additional factors which may influence the choice of vein.
7	Wash your hands with liquid soap and dry them.	To minimise the risk of healthcare-acquired infection.
8	Apply a tourniquet to the chosen site approximately 7–8cm above the puncture site. *Do not leave the tourniquet in place for any longer than 90 seconds (Lavery & Ingram 2005) as this will cause damage to the vein.* NB: To further encourage venous filling, you may wish to consider using the techniques described in Chapter 3 – for example, gently stroking the vein, or asking the patient to clench and unclench their fist.	To increase venous pressure to encourage filling of the vein.
9	Visually inspect and palpate the chosen vein.	To identify the depth and course of the vein, and to avoid nearby structures such as arteries and tendons.
10	Release the tourniquet to check that the vein has decompressed.	To reduce the length of time that the tourniquet is in place.
11	Wash your hands (or apply alcohol gel) thoroughly and put on gloves and apron.	To reduce the risk of healthcare-acquired infection.
12	Clean the patient's skin for 30 seconds. Allow to air-dry for a further 30 seconds. NB: *Do not touch or re-palpate the skin after cleansing has taken place, as this will contaminate the area.*	To reduce the risk of infection.

13	Re-apply the tourniquet.	
14	Apply traction to the skin 2–5cm below the proposed puncture site.	To anchor the vein, and facilitate the needle's entry.
15	Gather the needle and vacuum holder in your dominant hand and hold with your middle and index finger.	
16	Inspect the needle, ensuring that it is bevel up (the longer point of the needle will be seen closest to the skin).	To prevent the needle from advancing too far into the vein, and avoid inadvertently puncturing an artery.

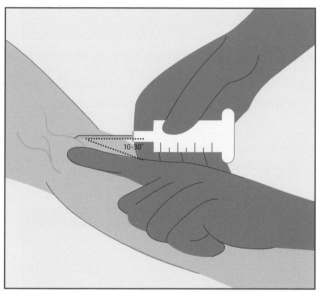

Figure 5.3: Insert the needle for venepuncture technique

17	Insert the needle at an angle of approximately 10–30 degrees (depending on the size and location of the vein selected).	To ensure appropriate filling of the blood collection tube.
18	Advance the needle 1–2 mm into the vein, maintaining a secure grip on the holder.	To reduce the risk of phlebitis and movement of the needle.
19	Attach the blood collection tube using your non-dominant hand. Push the tube into the syringe and twist clockwise to secure it.	

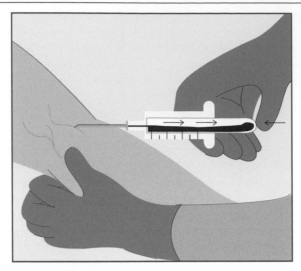

Figure 5.4: Introduce the vacuum tube into the holder

20	Allow time for filling of the blood collection tube. Once it has pre-filled to the required level, it will stop filling.	To prevent bleeding and haematoma formation.
21	Remove the tube from the needle. Repeat steps 19–21 until all the required blood samples have been obtained.	

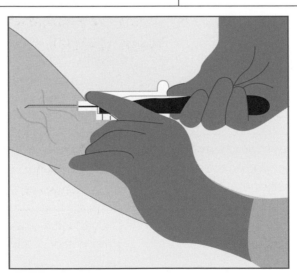

Figure 5.5: Remove the blood collection tube

22	Release the tourniquet once adequate blood flow has been achieved.	To prevent leakage of blood until the healing process is complete.

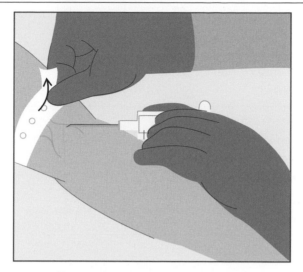

Figure 5.6: Undo the tourniquet

23	Apply a dry dressing over the puncture site; do not apply pressure until the needle has been removed. Apply pressure for approximately 2 minutes.	To avoid haematoma formation.

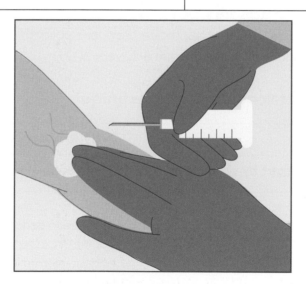

Figure 5.7: Apply pressure to the site

24	Place all sharps in a suitable container and dispose of them according to your local healthcare provider's policy.	To avoid needle-stick injury.

25 Ensure that the patient is comfortable. Advise them on whom to contact should the site start to bleed or become painful. You should also tell them to remove the dressing after 24 hours (if a dressing has been applied).	
26 Gently 'invert' (mix) each sample immediately after filling, as per the manufacturer's instructions. Complete the labelling on each sample taken, checking all details with the patient. Advise the patient when their blood results will be available.	

Following the correct venepuncture technique using a winged infusion device

If you are considering using a winged infusion device as an alternative to a vacuum system (for example, if your patient's veins are in poor condition, or you are required to take blood samples from a child), the steps are listed below:

NB: You will need to check your local healthcare provider's policy to ensure that this practice is supported prior to undertaking this (Ingram & Lavery 2009)

Table 5.2: Correct venepuncture technique using a winged device

What to do	Why it is done
Always start by washing your hands with soap and water.	
I Prepare the environment, thinking about the lighting and temperature.	To ensure that the practitioner is prepared to perform the procedure and that it can be carried out efficiently without interruption. This also ensures a safe working environment.
2 Gather all the equipment you will need, checking that the packaging is intact and none of the items has expired.	To ensure that the procedure is performed efficiently, safely and without distraction.

3	Identify the specific tests required on the requisition form and select the appropriate blood collection tubes and blood collection system.	To ensure that the correct samples are collected.
4	Identify the patient, checking their name band (where appropriate) or asking them to confirm their identity. Check these details against the blood requisition form. Check and confirm all details verbally with the patient.	To ensure that you have the correct patient.
5	Allow the patient time to ask any questions and provide information on how you will undertake the procedure.	To obtain the patient's consent and ensure their co-operation. Providing plenty of information will reduce their level of anxiety.
6	Determine the patient's preferred site for the procedure, based upon their previous experience, and ensure the patient's comfort once you have positioned them appropriately. For instance, they must be sitting comfortably and the arm must be supported (for example, using a pillow).	To maintain patient comfort, and to familiarise yourself with the patient's medical history and additional factors which may influence the choice of vein.
7	Wash your hands with liquid soap and dry them.	To minimise the risk of healthcare-acquired infection.
8	Apply a tourniquet to the chosen site approximately 7–8cm above the puncture site. *Do not leave the tourniquet in place for any longer than 90 seconds (Lavery & Ingram 2005) as this will cause damage to the vein.* NB: To further encourage venous filling, you may wish to consider using the techniques described in Chapter 3 – for example, gently stroking the vein, or asking the patient to clench and unclench their fist.	To increase venous pressure to encourage filling of the vein.
9	Visually inspect and palpate the chosen vein.	To identify the depth and course of the vein, and to avoid nearby structures such as arteries and tendons.

10	Release the tourniquet to check that the vein has decompressed.	To reduce the length of time that the tourniquet is in place.
11	Wash your hands (or apply alcohol gel) thoroughly and put on gloves and apron.	To reduce the risk of healthcare-acquired infection.
12	Clean the patient's skin for 30 seconds. Allow to air-dry for a further 30 seconds. NB: *Do not touch or re-palpate the skin after cleansing has taken place, as this will contaminate the area.*	To reduce the risk of healthcare-acquired infection.
13	Re-apply the tourniquet.	
14	Apply traction to the skin 2–5cm below the proposed puncture site.	To anchor the vein, and facilitate the needle's entry.
15	Assemble the winged device in your dominant hand and hold it with your thumb and index finger.	
16	Inspect the needle, ensuring that it is bevel up (the longer point of the needle will be seen closest to the skin).	To prevent the needle from advancing too far into the vein.
17	Insert the needle at an angle of approximately 5–15 degrees (depending on the size and location of the vein selected). Ensure that you insert the needle at a shallower angle than if you were using the traditional vacuum system.	To ensure appropriate filling of the blood collection tube.
18	Advance the needle 1mm into the vein, maintaining a secure grip on the holder.	
19	Flatten the wings of the butterfly device and secure with adhesive tape, or hold it in place with your non-dominant hand.	To prevent the device getting dislodged.
20	Observe for blood in the tubing, then attach the blood collection tube, using your non-dominant hand. Push the tube into the syringe and twist clockwise to secure it.	

21	Allow time for filling of the blood collection tube. Once it has pre-filled to the required level, it will stop filling.	
22	Remove the tube from the needle. Repeat steps 19–21 until all the required blood samples have been obtained.	
23	Release the tourniquet.	
24	Apply a dry dressing over the puncture site; do not apply pressure until the needle has been removed. Apply pressure for approximately 2 minutes.	To prevent localised infection at the puncture site.
25	Place all sharps in an appropriate container and dispose of them according to your local healthcare provider's policy.	To reduce the risk of a needle-stick injury.
26	Ensure that the patient is comfortable. Advise them on whom to contact should the site start to bleed or become painful. You should also tell them to remove the dressing after 24 hours (if a dressing has been applied).	To prevent leakage of blood until the healing process is complete.
27	Gently 'invert' (mix) each sample immediately after filling, as per manufacturer's instructions. Complete labelling on each sample taken, checking all details with the patient. Advise the patient when their blood results will be available.	

Caring for the puncture site

Once you have obtained your blood for analysis, you need to advise your patient about any aftercare that may be required for the puncture site. In most cases, once you have removed the needle, you can simply apply direct pressure to the site for a couple of minutes (or until the bleeding stops). If your patient has a blood clotting disorder, it may take longer to stop the bleed. To avoid any risk of infection, the site should be covered with a plaster or dry dressing after the procedure. Ensure that you document the care provided and any actions that you have taken, so that an accurate patient record is kept (NMC 2008).

Applying the principles of venepuncture to everyday practice

If you are new to venepuncture, you will need to be observed and assessed by a suitable qualified practitioner before you can be considered competent and able to perform the procedure independently. Many local healthcare providers have practical workbooks, which require you to document the number of attempts, the samples taken and record any problems noted. This can be used as your own evidence to support this clinical skill. Alternatively, you and your assessor can use the self-assessment checklist in Appendix 1 (see page 83) to support your practice.

Summary

In this chapter we have considered the practicalities of venepuncture, such as choosing an appropriate device to collect blood samples. We have highlighted the care of the puncture site and considered the 'order of draw' when collecting samples. You may want to undertake some further reading around specific requirements in relation to the particular blood samples that you are collecting.

Lastly, this chapter has discussed the step-by-step approach to taking blood samples, whether you are using a vacuum system or a winged infusion device. This procedure is not without risk, and there are many points to consider for your own practice. The following chapter gives guidance on what to do if complications arise during the venepuncture procedure.

Chapter 6

Venepuncture – when things go wrong

Learning outcomes

At the end of this chapter, the practitioner will be able to:

- Identify the common complications and problems that can occur with venepuncture
- Demonstrate the correct management of each of these complications.

There are many problems that can occur when undertaking venepuncture. This chapter looks at some of the most common potential problems and identifies some possible solutions.

It is important to recognise and manage any complications at the earliest opportunity, to ensure your patient's safety and to limit their pain and distress. Some of the common problems are identified below. You will need to read and understand this section before practising venepuncture on a patient for the first time.

Solving common problems and complications that can occur with venepuncture

What do I do if I am unsuccessful in obtaining a blood sample?

If you are unsuccessful in your attempt, this could be due to a number of different reasons. Most commonly, it will probably be due to poor vein assessment, an incorrect choice of sampling device or your own technique. Rarely, it may be due to faulty equipment, but this is unlikely. In order to prevent this problem, step back, concentrate on your vein assessment (for instance, ask yourself if another vein would be a better choice?) or could you perhaps use an alternative device? (for instance, could you consider using a winged infusion device if your patient has fragile veins?).

If you think you were unsuccessful because you are new to venepuncture, the cause may be your technique, so reflect on this and consider what you could do differently. Speak to the practitioner observing your practice and ask whether they can help you to identify what went wrong. Sometimes, practice makes perfect and it takes time to perfect your technique. Whatever the reason, you will need to release the tourniquet, remove the vacuum bottle and needle, and start the procedure again. If you are unsuccessful, you should only have two attempts at different sites before asking a more experienced practitioner to help you (Perruca 2001).

What do I do if I have collected an incomplete sample?

If you get blood initially but then the blood collection tube stops filling, it could be due to one of the reasons listed in the table opposite.

What do I do if I notice a haematoma?

A haematoma is caused by blood leaking from the blood vessel into the surrounding tissues at the puncture site. The common reasons for a haematoma occurring are either poor technique or inserting the needle through the vein wall to the opposite side (as discussed in Table 6.1). Haematomas can also be caused by applying inadequate pressure to the puncture site after the procedure, or by not removing the tourniquet before removing the needle. In such cases, you need to consider your venepuncture technique and work to improve it.

If a haematoma occurs during the procedure, release the tourniquet, remove the blood collection tube and needle, and apply direct pressure to the puncture site. You will need to start the procedure again, using an alternative site and new equipment.

Ensure that you document in the patient's notes what has happened. You should also advise the patient to monitor the site and inform medical staff straight away in case of severe pain, worsening symptoms, or if they are generally concerned about the area for any reason.

Table 6.1: Reasons for incomplete blood sample collection

Problem	Prevention	Action
You may have inserted the needle through the vein wall on the opposite side.	Consider the angle of needle entry – it may have been too deep.	Withdraw the needle slightly to encourage withdrawal of the blood. If you see bruising, release the tourniquet, and remove the needle and vacuum bottle. Apply pressure to the puncture point and start the procedure again.
The needle may be in contact with a valve.	Ensure that you carry out accurate vein assessment and palpation of the vein. (The valve feels like a raised nodule.)	Withdraw the needle slightly to move it away from the valve. If this does not work, release the tourniquet, remove the needle and vacuum bottle fully and start the procedure again.
There is a venous spasm.	This normally occurs as a result of mechanical irritation.	Massage the vein above the point of entry. This can occasionally be resolved by removing, and applying a new blood bottle. If you are using a winged infusion device, attach a syringe to the device to reduce the vacuum pressure.
The vein collapses.	The tourniquet may have been applied too tightly.	Release the tourniquet and allow the vein to re-fill.
The vein used is too small.	Accurate vein assessment will ensure that you select a suitable vein. Choose a more appropriately sized vein next time.	Consider using a smaller gauge needle or a winged collection device, as this can be angled much closer to the skin. Using a syringe attachment may reduce the pressure on the vein (Phillips, Collins & Dougherty 2011).

What do I do if I have accidentally punctured an artery?

If you have punctured an artery, you will be able to identify arterial blood from the colour, consistency and the frequency of leakage from the site. Bright red blood will be seen pulsating within the blood collection system. In this case, remove the blood collection system, release the tourniquet and remove the needle immediately. Apply direct pressure to the site for a good 5 minutes, or until the bleeding has stopped. Apply a pressure dressing to the site for at least 10–15 minutes. Make sure that you report arterial puncture to medical staff. Once you are satisfied that the bleeding has stopped, the pressure dressing can be removed and a dry dressing applied. You will need to monitor the site for 24 hours. Make sure that you document the incident in the patient's notes, and advise the patient to monitor the site and inform medical staff in case of any problems such as bleeding starting again.

What do I do if I have hit a nerve?

If you have hit a nerve, the patient will let you know very quickly! Hitting a nerve is uncommon but may be caused by poor patient assessment and inappropriate angle of needle insertion. Release the tourniquet, remove the needle and apply direct pressure to the puncture site. You will need to re-start the procedure, using a different vein and clean equipment.

What do I do if I notice bruising around the site?

Bruising is caused by a leakage of blood into the tissues, and is often due to poor venepuncture technique or due to the fact that the patient bleeds easily (RCN 2010). For example, elderly patients, those with fragile veins and those on medication that can affect blood clotting may show signs of bruising.

There are many easy ways to avoid bruising the patient:

- Consider your venepuncture technique, and ensure that you take a confident approach.
- Take care to identify the most suitable vein from which to collect your blood samples.
- Take care to check your angle of needle insertion.
- Do not apply the tourniquet too tightly.
- 'Fix' the vein into position using your other hand and by using skin traction when inserting the needle.
- Ensure that you apply adequate pressure to the puncture site after removal of the needle to prevent further damage (Campbell 1995).

What do I do if my patient complains of excessive pain?

This may be caused by frequent use of the same vein, a poor technique, hitting a nerve or a valve, or lastly if the patient is anxious. You can prevent excessive pain by ensuring that your patient is relaxed and comfortable, and that the arm is appropriately supported on pillows. If your patient is known to be anxious, you may need someone to reassure them whilst you carry out the procedure. You may want to consider using a local anaesthetic cream where appropriate. (This will need to be prescribed according to your local healthcare provider's prescribing policy.)

You also need to consider your own technique, and carry out the procedure in a confident, unhurried manner in order to reassure the patient. You should have a good working knowledge of the structure of the veins, arteries and surrounding nerves and tissues to ensure that you can assess the appropriate site and the vein correctly.

What do I do to avoid the risk of phlebitis?

Phlebitis is defined as an inflammation of the vein, and is characterised by redness, pain and swelling. It is a rare complication in venepuncture but can potentially be caused by mechanical methods (the needle rubbing inside the vein) or because the practitioner has adopted a poor aseptic technique. Phlebitis can be avoided by following the correct working practices in relation to infection control, and maintaining a 'non-touch' technique at the venepuncture site throughout the procedure. For example, do not re-palpate the vein after you have cleansed the site, as this can potentially cause infective phlebitis.

Summary

In this chapter we have considered the common complications and problems that can be encountered with venepuncture. This will give you some insight into what to do if things go wrong. As you will see from the problems listed above, there is often very little that you can do to rectify the problem, except to release the tourniquet, remove the needle and start the procedure again.

You may also want to read Chapter 10, which focuses on risk, infection control and health and safety in relation to both venepuncture and cannulation

Chapter 7

Cannulation

Learning outcomes

At the end of this chapter, the practitioner will be able to:

- Choose a device, identifying the correct size and use
- Identify the equipment needed to perform the procedure
- Care for the cannula following insertion.

As always, it is important to make sure that you follow your local healthcare provider's policy before undertaking cannulation. Some local policies and guidelines are very detailed; and may include a rationale and step-by-step approach to performing the procedure. In addition, there are published articles that will provide you with a detailed understanding of the important processes to be considered when performing cannulation.

Activity

Find and read your local healthcare provider's cannulation policy or guidelines. Make sure that you understand and adopt the working practices detailed in them before undertaking this role.

Choosing a cannula

When considering choosing a cannula, you will probably be limited to a specific manufacturer that is used by your local healthcare provider. There are various cannula designs on the market, made of PVC or polyurethane materials. Polyurethane materials have become more common in recent years; they are softer, cause less vein damage and are kink-resistant, which reduces the incidence of cannula failure. Some cannula designs have 'wings' to help secure the device to the skin, others have ports (these are known as 'ported cannulas') to allow the additional administration of medication. Many cannula designs now incorporate an additional safety feature to reduce the risk of needle-stick injury. The nurse can activate the safety feature by pressing a button or, more typically, putting in the needle stylet. The stylet has a shielding facility, which is automatically activated on removal from the cannula (RCN 2010).

There are a range of cannula sizes (gauges) available, so it is important to think about why you need to use the device. As discussed in Chapter 1, there are many reasons for needing a cannula. Identifying the specific reason should help you to consider the site and gauge needed, as well as where the cannula will be located. Many manufacturers have colour-coded cannulas so you can easily identify what size gauge you need to use. This is not completely standardised, so you will need to check with the manufacturer used by your local healthcare provider. Remember, you should always insert the smallest cannula possible to avoid damage to the vein, and allow administered medicines or therapies to 'mix' with the blood (Hadaway & Millam 2005). A smaller cannula will also be more comfortable for the patient, which is an equally important consideration.

Table 7.1: Cannula colour, size, flow rate and purpose

Gauge	Manufacturer colour	Flow rate (approx.)	Used for
22g	Blue	40ml/min	Small, fragile veins, short-term access
20g	Pink	65ml/min	Routine infusions, post operatively, bolus drug administration
18g	Green	100ml/min	Routine blood transfusion, rapid infusion, surgical/trauma patient
16g	Grey	210ml/min	Major trauma or surgery, massive fluid replacement
14g	Brown	270ml/min	Emergency

As a rule of thumb, a small-gauge cannula provides a flow rate that is sufficient to deliver most treatment therapies, and also reduces the risk of complications for your patient (this is discussed in more detail in Chapter 10).

Activity

Look at the types of cannula used in your practice area. What is the gauge range and flow rate for each cannula that is used?

Identifying the equipment required for cannulation

Having assessed the patient and selected the correct device, you need to gather all the required equipment before undertaking the procedure. Many local healthcare providers have cannulation packs that are specially designed to contain everything you need to be fully prepared to undertake the procedure.

Use this checklist to make sure that you gather all the required equipment:

- Personal protective equipment (such as appropriately sized clean gloves and apron)
- A tourniquet, ideally 'single-use' (disposable)
- A clean tray or receiver
- Appropriately sized cannula – you will need two cannulas in case the first attempt is unsuccessful
- Swabs to clean the insertion site, either alcohol-based or antiseptic, depending on your local healthcare provider's policy
- Protective cover to avoid any blood spilling on your patient
- A sharps bin or container should be close at hand
- Gauze swabs
- Adhesive tape
- Sterile occlusive (see-through) dressing
- 10mL syringe containing 0.9% sodium chloride – to flush the cannula after insertion. (NB: The sodium chloride flush must be prescribed by an authorised prescriber, or through a patient group directive if it is supported. For unregistered

practitioners, your local healthcare provider's policy will allow flushing of the cannula immediately after insertion to assess patency (check that the cannula is unobstructed). This is often accepted as an inherent part of the procedure. However, this is the only circumstance in which unregistered practitioners may perform this practice. Make sure that you check your local healthcare provider's policy or guidelines for confirmation.)

Make sure that all the packaging is in date and intact prior to use. If it is damaged or out of date, discard immediately.

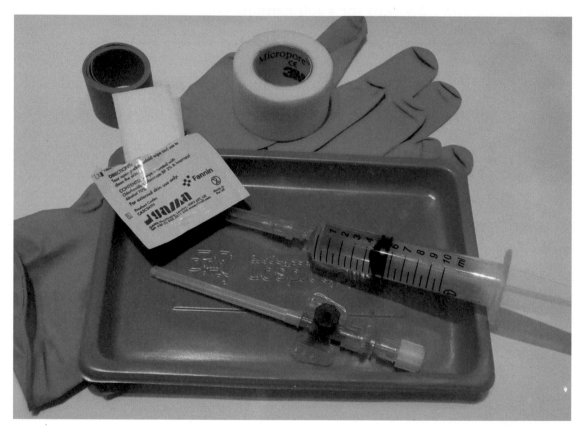

Figure 7.1: Equipment required for cannulation

Cannulation technique will be discussed in detail in the next chapter but it is important for the practitioner to document all information as soon as the procedure has been performed. Good record-keeping is an integral part of professional practice (NMC 2009), with records sometimes potentially being used as evidence in court as part of an investigation or patient complaint. Your records should also document when care of the cannula has been undertaken.

Documentation following cannula insertion should include:

- Patient information and type of consent given (for example, implied, verbal or written)
- Date/time and location of cannula insertion (for instance, antecubital fossa on the left arm)
- Size/type of cannula used (many manufacturers include a pre-printed label that contains this information and batch number, which must be inserted in the patient's notes to provide a clear record, this is a Medicines and Healthcare products Regulatory Agency requirement, as it is a medical device indwelling in the patient)
- Details of the type of dressing applied to the cannula site
- Any problems with the procedure noted.

Many local healthcare providers now have a pre-printed cannula care pathway with different sections for the practitioner to complete following insertion. There is usually space to write about the daily cannula care provided and to record a phlebitis score. Phlebitis scoring is discussed in more detail in Chapter 10. If you do not have access to a cannula care pathway, make sure that you consider the information above when completing the patient's notes.

Activity

Find a patient with a cannula in your practice setting and look at their patient notes. What does the documentation say? Can you clearly identify when the cannula was inserted? Is there a care plan for the cannula while it is in place?

Caring for the cannula following insertion

The Standards for Infusion Therapy (RCN 2010) include a standard on cannula site care and maintenance, which is well worth reading. Many local healthcare providers have devised their own guidelines for cannula care, which usually form part of their cannula care pathway. The Department of Health (DH 2007, 2010) have said that, when performing cannula site care, the practitioner should also observe the device and surrounding area, as well as evaluating the integrity of the device and the security of any connections.

The guidance below provides the practitioner with a minimum standard to care for and maintain a cannula:

Table 7.2: Caring for a cannula

What to do	Why it is done
Inspect the cannula each shift (or more frequently if the patient's clinical condition dictates it).	To ensure correct cannula position.
The RCN (2010) recommends that a cannula should be re-sited every 72–96 hours.	To observe for potential complications.
Flush the cannula with 0.9% sodium chloride at established intervals (e.g. before and after each use of the cannula) or every 24 hours if it is not in use, using an aseptic non-touch technique (ANNT). *NB: you will need to have had additional training in the preparation and administration of intravenous drugs in order to flush a cannula.*	To maintain patency of the cannula.
Adopt an ANNT when handling the cannula/infusion sets, and avoid any break in the infusion system. A closed system should be used to minimise the risk of infection	A break in the infusion system could allow contamination to enter the circulatory system.
Secure the cannula with a semi-permeable cannula dressing.	To reduce the risk of mechanical complications such as the cannula being dislodged.
Apply a transparent dressing.	To allow for visual inspection of the cannula site.
Avoid replacing the dressing unless it is visually soiled or damaged.	To reduce the risk of infection to the cannula site or dislodging of the device.

Activity

Identify a patient within your practice area who is receiving an infusion of IV fluids for rehydration purposes. Decide where you would insert a cannula and consider what size you would use. Think about the reasons on which you have based your decision.

Summary

In this chapter we have considered some of the practical issues involved with intravenous cannulation. We have covered identifying the correct device and size, as well as ensuring that the cannula selected fits the clinical needs of the patient. We have considered the correct equipment required to perform the procedure, as well as caring for the cannula following insertion.

Chapter 8

Cannulation technique

Learning outcomes

At the end of this chapter, the practitioner will be able to:

- Understand correct cannulation technique
- Re-site a cannula if necessary
- Remove a cannula
- Apply principles of cannulation to practice.

Once you have prepared the necessary equipment, yourself, your environment and your patient, you need to gain a knowledge of cannulation technique. Cannulation can take some time to master but practice does make perfect in the end! The patient's comfort and safety should always be your prime concern and the golden rule is that you should make no more than two attempts at the procedure (Perucca 2001). If you are still unsuccessful, ask a more experienced practitioner to perform the procedure for you. The key stages of the cannulation procedure are identified in the table below.

Table 8.1: The key stages of cannulation

What to do	Why it is done
Always start by washing your hands with soap and water.	
1 Prepare the environment, thinking about the lighting and temperature.	To ensure that the practitioner is prepared to perform the procedure and that it can be carried out efficiently without interruption.
2 Gather all the equipment you will need, checking that the packaging is intact and none of the items has expired.	To ensure that the procedure is performed efficiently, safely and without distraction.
3 Check the patient's identity. Ask the patient their name and date of birth and check these details against identification (e.g. hospital name band or documentation).	To ensure that you have the correct patient (NPSA 2006).
4 Position the patient on a bed or chair, and ensure that they are comfortable and relaxed. Explain the procedure and allow them time to ask questions and raise any concerns. Ask them if they have had a cannula in before. Check whether there were any problems associated with the procedure. Identify which arm they would prefer (use the non-dominant hand where possible) and support the limb appropriately. Apply topical local anaesthetic if requested by the patient.	To obtain the patient's consent and ensure their co-operation. Providing plenty of information will reduce their level of anxiety. To maintain patient comfort, and to familiarise yourself with the patient's medical history and additional factors which may influence the choice of vein.
5 Apply a tourniquet (ideally 'single use') 7–8cm above the cannula insertion site. Use alternative methods to encourage venous filling if required (e.g. warming the limb, clenching the fist, etc.). *Do not leave the tourniquet in place for any longer than 90 seconds (Lavery & Ingram 2005) as this will cause damage to the vein.*	To encourage filling of the vein (RCN 2010), and help make the vein more prominent.

6	Visually inspect the patient's veins, and palpate to identify and select the most appropriate site. Release the tourniquet after you have identified a suitable vein. Leave the tourniquet loosely in place.	To promote a successful procedure at your first attempt.
7	Open equipment packs ready to perform the procedure and prepare the area.	
8	Wash your hands again with soap and water.	To ensure that you are ready and prepared to carry out the procedure.
9	Clean the patient's skin for 30 seconds. Allow to air-dry for a minimum of 30 seconds. NB: *Do not touch or re-palpate the skin after cleansing has taken place, as this will contaminate the area.*	To minimise the risk of healthcare-acquired infection (RCN 2010).
10	Tighten the tourniquet to the proposed puncture site.	To prevent stinging on insertion of the cannula.
11	Put on gloves and apron.	
12	Remove the needle guard and inspect the cannula to ensure that there are no faults. Hold the device firmly.	To ensure that the equipment is not faulty (RCN 2010).
13	Ensure that the needle is bevel up (the longer point of the needle will be seen closest to the skin).	To ease the cannula's entry.
14	Anchor the vein by applying tension to the skin below the cannulation site.	To prevent the vein from moving during the procedure. To facilitate smooth needle entry (Phillips, Collins & Dougherty 2011).
15	Insert the device at an angle (between 10 and 40 degrees). Fragile veins will require a lower angle of insertion.	Primary flashback indicates that the cannula is inserted into the vein.

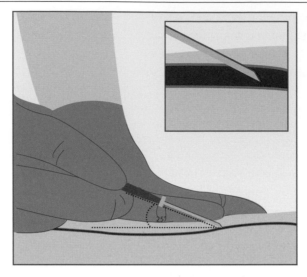

Figure 8.1: Insert the cannula

16	Wait for the flashback to appear in the chamber of the cannula. Lower the angle of the cannula and advance a few millimetres into the vein. Avoid contamination of the device by holding the wings of the cannula, or the protective cap	To ensure that venous access is maintained.

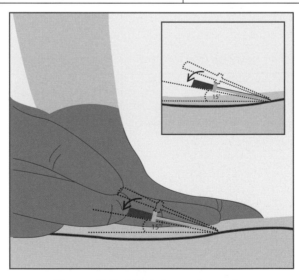

Figure 8.2: Withdraw the stylet

17	Withdraw stylet a few millimetres and wait for secondary flashback (seen along the cannula shaft).	To ensure that the cannula is in the correct position and can be inserted into the lumen of the vein.

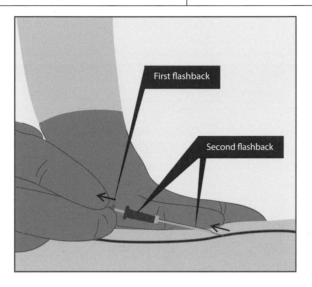

Figure 8.3: Withdraw the stylet

18	Advance the cannula forward off the needle and into the vein with your other hand in one smooth movement. You need to ensure that the vein remains anchored during this part of the procedure.	To find out if any resistance is being experienced. The cannula should advance easily. If not, you may need to remove it and place a new cannula in a different vein.

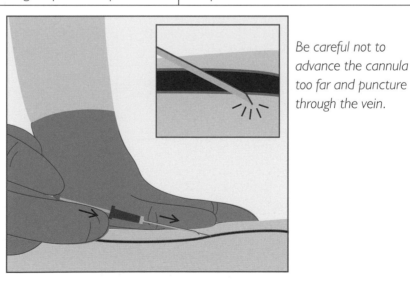

Be careful not to advance the cannula too far and puncture through the vein.

Figure 8.4: Advance the cannula

19	Release the tourniquet.	To release venous pressure.
20	Apply pressure over the vein at the cannula tip (ensure that the cannula is anchored).	To prevent blood spillage.
21	Remove the stylet and dispose of it in the sharps bin.	To prevent needle-stick injury.

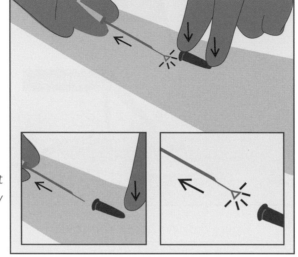

Remove the stylet carefully

If a needle safety device is used, the needle will retract automatically to reduce the risk of needle stick injury

Figure 8.5: Remove the stylet

22	Connect the intravenous giving set or the intravenous bung to the end of the cannula.	To prevent blood spillage and bacteria entry to the site.
23	Flush the cannula with 10mL of 0.9% sodium chloride using a push–pause method. (NB: Observe for signs of swelling or leakage. Ask the patient if it feels uncomfortable or painful.)	To confirm correct placement, and to ensure patency of the cannula.
24	Secure the cannula in position with an appropriate dressing.	To reduce irritation to the vein and secure the device.
25	Remove gloves and apron.	To prevent cross-contamination.
26	Dispose of all clinical waste as per your local health provider's clinical waste policy.	To ensure that you are complying with universal precautions.

27	Provide your patient with after-care advice.	To ensure compliance.
28	Document the procedure using a cannula care pathway. If this is not available, document the date, time, size and location of the cannula. Record and print your name and designation.	To ensure accountability and good record keeping (NMC 2008).

Remember that you should have no more than two attempts at cannulation, using a different site each time, and providing the patient is happy for you to have a second attempt. If after two attempts you are still unsuccessful, you must ask a more experienced colleague to perform the procedure.

If all goes well, by taking the time to perform an accurate patient assessment and selection of an appropriate vein, you will be able to perform cannulation successfully first time.

Having said that, sometimes things do go wrong. Read the next chapter to inform yourself about the potential complications of cannulation if you encounter a problem during or after the procedure.

Re-siting a cannula

Your local healthcare provider's policy will probably advise you on what to do if a cannula requires re-siting. Make sure that you follow the same steps as the initial insertion of a cannula, described in Table 8.1 above.

A cannula may need re-siting because:

● It has been in place for 72–96 hours (RCN 2010)

● The site has become infected

● Or the cannula is blocked or leaking around the site.

If you need to re-site a cannula, make sure that you choose a different vein (ideally on an alternate limb if possible). If you have to use the same limb for clinical reasons, make sure the new site is above (proximal) to the previous one. Rotation of cannula sites is essential, but there may be some restrictions owing to the patient's condition, previous medical history or their mobility. Make sure that you document the reason for removal, and record whether there were any complications (such as phlebitis or blockage).

Removing a cannula safely

Before removing a cannula, you will need to ensure that your patient is prepared and that you have explained the procedure to them. Equally important is explaining the after-care of the cannulation site. The RCN (2010) recommend that peripheral intravenous devices should be re-sited every 72–96 hours.

To remove a cannula, you will need the following equipment:

● Gloves/apron

● Clean tray

● Sharps bin

● Gauze swab (cotton wool is no longer recommended due to the risk of cotton fibres entering the circulatory system)

● Sterile dressing/plaster to cover the cannulation site (plus adhesive tape if needed)

● Protective cover in case of blood spillage.

It is very simple to remove a cannula. First, ensure that all intravenous therapy has ended and that the cannula is no longer required. Then follow the steps in the table below to ensure successful removal.

Table 8.2: The key stages of removing a cannula

What to do	Why it is done
1 Wash your hands, and put on gloves and apron.	To reduce the risk of healthcare-acquired infection and contamination of your hands from blood
2 If an infusion is running, close the flow clamp and discontinue the infusion.	To prevent leakage of fluid.
3 Remove the dressing from the cannula using ANNT. Take care not to pull or dislodge the cannula at this stage.	
4 Gently remove the cannula and use a gauze swab over the cannulation site to apply pressure.	

5 After removal, apply pressure to the site for 2–3 minutes or until the bleeding stops.	To avoid the risk of the site re-bleeding, which can occur if pressure is not applied for long enough
6 Cover the site with a dry dressing or plaster (check that the patient is not allergic to the product prior to use).	To prevent infection from entering the puncture site.
7 Check that the cannula is not damaged and is complete. Discard into a sharps bin. If there are signs of infection present, report this to medical staff, as the cannula tip may require microbiological investigation.	To avoid the risk of any part being left in the patient, and to avoid the risk of needle-stick injury. To monitor peripheral device-related bacteraemia.
8 Document the date and time of removal as well as any problems encountered.	To ensure good record-keeping practice (NMC 2008).

Summary

This chapter has discussed a step-by-step approach to the insertion, care and removal of a cannula. You will need to be observed and assessed by a practitioner who is qualified to undertake this role before you can be considered competent and able to perform cannulation independently. You can use the self-assessment checklist (see Appendix 2, p. 85) to support your practice.

The procedure is not without risk, and there are many points to remember for your practice, so you will probably need to re-read this chapter to refresh your knowledge. The next chapter identifies some of the common complications associated with a cannula once it has been sited.

Chapter 9

Cannulation – when things go wrong

Learning outcomes

At the end of this chapter, the practitioner will be able to:

- Identify the common complications and problems that can occur with cannulation
- Demonstrate the correct management of each of these complications.

There are many common problems or potential complications associated with cannulation. This chapter seeks to identify some of these, and provide the practitioner with some solutions if they arise. It is important to remember that the potential for any complication to occur can be associated with some of the contributing factors discussed in detail in Chapter 3, such as the patient's age, gender, weight gain/loss, any disease, and the skill level of the practitioner performing the procedure.

Any complications need to be recognised and managed at the earliest opportunity, as they can cause the patient pain and distress. Some of the common complications at the insertion stage are identified in the section below. You will need to read this section before practising your cannulation technique on a patient for the first time. Other complications can occur once the cannula is in place, and these are also described in detail in this chapter.

Solving common problems and complications that can occur with cannulation

What do I do if I've missed the vein when trying to insert a cannula?

This can be due to many reasons, such as inadequate anchoring of the vein, vein collapse, poor vein choice, incorrect insertion angle or incorrect position of the patient. To avoid these problems, it is important to consider your preparation and level of concentration when performing the procedure. It is equally important to adopt a good cannulation technique. If you have missed a vein, you may be able to rectify the situation by slightly withdrawing the needle and re-aligning it (if your patient is happy for you to do this, as it may cause some pain). If this is unsuccessful, you will need to remove the cannula and start the procedure again, using a new cannula and selecting an alternative vein.

What do I do if I don't get an initial flashback?

Again, there may be a variety of reasons for this but typically the angle of entry into the vein may not be deep enough. This is a common problem when starting out, so think about your cannulation technique. If this happens, slowly advance your needle and look out for the flashback. If you still don't get a flashback, you need to remove the cannula and start again, using a new cannula and a different vein. If you get a flashback but it is a very small amount of blood, this might be because you are using a small-gauge cannula. Make sure that you allow at least 20 seconds for the flashback to appear.

What do I do if there is no secondary flashback?

If you don't get a secondary flashback, this is often due to one of two reasons: either you have not penetrated the vein deeply enough, or you have punctured the vein wall through both sides. Consider your technique and angle of insertion, and try manipulating the cannula slightly. Lower the angle of insertion to ensure that your needle enters the centre of the lumen of the vein. If you still have no success, remove the cannula and start the procedure again, using a new cannula and a different vein.

What do I do if there is blood leaking around the needle on entry?

This normally happens because you are too slow in advancing the stylet. You need to consider your cannulation technique and work to improve it. You need to be more confident in your approach. Also, consider whether your tourniquet is too tight. In either scenario, the cannula will need removing and re-siting, using a new cannula and a different vein.

What do I do if I have hit a nerve?

If you have hit a nerve, the patient will let you know very quickly! This is an uncommon complication that is often caused by poor assessment of the veins and an inappropriate angle of cannula insertion. There is very little that you can do, except to remove the cannula immediately and apply pressure to the site to stop the bleeding. You will need to re-site the cannula, using new equipment and a different vein. Monitor the patient closely for feelings of reduced sensation in the area, and inform medical staff. Your patient may require analgesia for pain. In the worst-case scenario, your patient may require physiotherapy for the affected area if there is persistent nerve damage. Make sure that the incident is documented in the patient's notes. You will also need to complete a clinical incident form.

What do I do if a haematoma has formed at the cannula site?

A haematoma occurs when only the uppermost wall of the vein is punctured, or if you have removed the tourniquet after trying to remove the needle. This is a fairly common problem when first starting out, as practitioners often forget to remove the tourniquet! Using the major veins can help, as can adopting a good cannulation technique. If you do see a haematoma form when you are inserting a cannula, remove the cannula straight away and apply pressure to the site. Re-site the cannula, using new equipment and another limb.

What do I do if I have accidentally punctured an artery?

If you have punctured an artery, you will be able to identify arterial blood from the colour, consistency and the rate at which it is leaking from the site. Bright red blood will be seen pulsating within the flashback chamber. If you have punctured an artery, remove the cannula (see section below on removing a cannula safely) and apply direct pressure to the site for a good 5 minutes, or until the bleeding has stopped. Apply a pressure dressing to the site for at least 10–15 minutes. Make sure that your report the arterial puncture to medical staff. Once they are satisfied that the bleeding has stopped, the pressure bandage can be removed and a dry dressing applied. You will need to monitor the site closely for at least 24 hours. Make sure that the incident is recorded in the patient's notes. You will also need to complete a clinical incident form

What do I do if fluid is leaking around the insertion site when I flush the cannula?

Sometimes this can happen even when you think the procedure is going well. Fluid accumulating around the insertion site may indicate that the cannula is in the subcutaneous tissue and not in the vein. In this case, you need to remove the cannula straight away and start the procedure again, using a new cannula and a different vein.

What do I do if I have difficulty advancing the cannula, and I can feel some resistance?

This may be due to the fact that you have removed the stylet too far, and this means that the cannula is not rigid enough to advance any further. Using a good angle of approach can prevent this. Take care when advancing the cannula from the stylet. Another consideration is that you may have hit a valve, in which case you will need to remove the cannula and start the procedure again with new equipment and using a different vein.

What do I do if I have been unsuccessful in inserting the cannula?

Unsuccessful insertion may be due to poor technique, and it is fairly common when starting out. Normally, the angle of insertion is wrong, with the practitioner going into the vein too steeply at the beginning of the procedure. Alternatively, it may be due to the poor condition of the patient's veins. Careful patient assessment and an adequate level of supervision are essential when learning this procedure to ensure that you are competent to perform it. Remember to follow your local healthcare provider's policy and procedure to achieve safe practice. If you are unsuccessful at your first attempt, remove the cannula and re-site, using a new cannula and a different vein. Ensure that you anchor the patient's vein sufficiently when inserting a new cannula, as this will help to stabilise the vein.

What do I do if the cannula is damaged?

Very rarely will you open a cannula packet and find it damaged. Damage is more likely to occur if the needle has been re-sheathed into the cannula itself. Make sure that you never re-sheath the needle. When flushing the cannula to confirm patency, ensure that you do not use a syringe smaller than 10mL, as the pressure build-up from using a smaller syringe can cause sufficient internal pressure to rupture the device.

Dealing with phlebitis associated with cannulation

There are many specific patient infections that can be caused by intravenous cannulation, and these often occur once the cannula is in place. The most common is infective phlebitis. Infective phlebitis can potentially cause septicaemia, so it is important that you update your knowledge on this topic and that you are aware of the signs and symptoms.

Phlebitis is defined as inflammation of the vein, and is characterised by redness, pain and swelling (Dougherty 2008). It is estimated that up to 80% of patients receiving intravenous therapy have reported signs and symptom of phlebitis (Ung, Cook, Edwards, Hocking, Osmond & Buttergieg 2002), showing that it is a common problem within clinical practice. There are three types of phlebitis – mechanical, chemical and infective. All types of phlebitis can be prevented by the careful selection of the vein and the device, and use of an aseptic non-touch technique (ANNT) when performing the procedure.

Mechanical phlebitis

This happens because the cannula itself causes inflammation to the Tunica Intima section of the vein. To reduce the risk of mechanical phlebitis, it is recommended that the smallest-gauge cannula be used (Scales 2005).

Infective phlebitis

This is caused by infection entering the cannula site and can be attributed to poor cannulation technique. It is important that you adopt ANNT, and make sure that your needle stays sterile to reduce the risk of infection.

Chemical phlebitis

This is due to the administered fluid or medication causing inflammation of the vein. Make sure that the correct strength of the infusion is administered at the preparation stage.

It is essential that effective cannula care is maintained once the device is in place, and that you are able to recognise the signs and symptoms of phlebitis, which are as follows:

- Redness at the cannula site
- Pain at the site or along the path of the cannula
- Swelling
- Induration (hardening)
- Pyrexia (high temperature)

- Palpable venous cord (when the vein feels like a hard cord under the skin and is often tender to the touch).

Many local healthcare providers have now adopted the use of a phlebitis scale to assist practitioners with a cannula checking procedure. Although there are various phlebitis scales that have been published, the RCN (2010) Guidelines for Infusion Therapy have adopted Jackson (1998) as the preferred risk assessment tool. This has a scoring system ranging from 0 (no signs of phlebitis) to 5 (advanced stage thrombophlebitis) and provides the practitioner with a management plan depending upon the score. This includes removal of the device, and symptom control. The Department of Health advocate the use of a visual phlebitis tool as a care bundle for peripheral IV cannula care (DH 2010)

The RCN (2010) guidelines also suggest that practitioners follow the points below in order to reduce the incidence of infusion phlebitis.

Points for your practice

- **Observe the cannula site at least daily (recommended good practice would be to increase this frequency to two or three times daily)**
- **Secure the cannula with an intravenous dressing (semi-occlusive)**
- **Replace loose, contaminated dressings**
- **Insert the cannula away from joints wherever possible**
- **Use an aseptic non-touch technique**
- **Re-site the cannula every 72–96 hours (or when clinically indicated)**
- **Plan and document care**
- **Use the smallest-gauge cannula suitable for patient need**
- **Replace the cannula at the first sign of infusion phlebitis.**

Jackson's (1998) phlebitis risk assessment tool (updated 2008) can be found in: RCN (2010). *Standards for Infusion Therapy*. London: RCN (see Appendix 1).

Jackson, A. (1998). Infection control: a battle in vein infusion phlebitis. *Nursing Times*. **94** (4), 68–71.

Activity

Search for your local healthcare provider's phlebitis risk assessment tool (often referred to as the VIP tool) and read it. Select a patient with a cannula in place (or 'in situ') and practise scoring using the assessment tool.

The Department of Health (2010) publication, 'High impact intervention: peripheral IV cannula care', makes reference to the use of a visual phlebitis score through the use of care bundles. This document can be accessed through the Department of Health website: http://webarchive.nationalarchives.gov.uk/20120118164404/hcai.dh.gov.uk/files/2011/03/2011-03-14-HII-Peripheral-intravenous-cannula-bundle-FIN%e2%80%a6.pdf

Dealing with infiltration and extravasation

Infiltration or extravasation is more commonly known in clinical practice as cannula 'tissuing'. Infiltration is the inadvertent administration of a non-vesicant fluid or medication into surrounding tissues, whereas extravasation is the inadvertent administration of a vesicant (a chemical substance) fluid/solution into the surrounding tissues. Examples of vesicant medications include Vancomycin, Potassium Chloride and Dopamine. The signs and symptoms of infiltration and extravasation are not always obvious until a few hours after the patient's cannula has failed. This usually depends on how rapidly the medication or fluid is being infused.

Signs and symptoms of infiltration and extravasation include swelling at the insertion site, cooling and blanching of the skin, and leakage around the cannula. The patient may also complain of pain and this is usually related to the amount of swelling at the insertion site. Extravasation can also appear as redness around the affected site, similar to sunburn.

Sometimes the patient may complain of a burning sensation and this will need immediate assessment, as it may indicate that tissue necrosis is occurring. This can lead to long-term problems, with the potential need for surgical removal of the necrosed tissue. The degree of tissue damage will depend on the type of drug or fluid being infused and how long it is present in the tissues before being discovered. Both complications usually cause the slowing or stopping of the infusion, which is often the first sign that there is a problem with the cannula. Prompt action needs to be taken, as this is potentially a critical incident.

Infiltration and extravasation are often due to poor site selection, especially if the cannula is inserted over a joint. A traumatic cannula insertion can damage the lining of the vein, thus predisposing it to further damage when an irritating fluid or medication is infused. It is therefore important to adopt good cannulation technique. For instance, once the cannula has been inserted, it must be adequately secured. If it is inadequately secured, it can move around, and this could cause the tip to go through the vein wall and infuse medication or fluid into the surrounding tissues. It is also vital that an appropriate dressing is selected and used when performing the procedure.

Treatment options for infiltration and extravasation should be commenced at the first sign of a problem. If an infusion is running, this should be stopped immediately. If the therapy is still required, the cannula should be re-sited on another limb.

Dealing with bruising

Bruising is a common complication and it occurs when blood leaks into tissues. This may be due to the practitioner's poor technique during the procedure, medication that alters blood clotting, or the fact that some patients tend to bleed easily (such as those with fragile veins). One strategy to avoid this in patients with poor-quality veins is to apply a blood pressure cuff to the limb, to 'fill' the vein, rather than a tourniquet. If you see bruising at the cannula site, release the tourniquet, remove the cannula and apply pressure on the puncture site immediately.

Another potential complication of cannulation is kinking of the cannula. This is common when the cannula is positioned at a joint (such as the elbow). In this situation, you should remove the cannula and apply pressure on the puncture site, then start again using a new cannula and an alternative site.

Summary

As we have seen in this chapter, there are many complications that can arise either when inserting a cannula or once the device is in place. It is therefore essential that you have a good understanding of any potential complications, so that you can manage them if they arise. You may find it helpful to read around this subject in more detail, as there is plenty of information available (see Further Reading, p. 88).

Chapter 10

Reducing risks when carrying out venepuncture and cannulation

Learning outcomes

At the end of this chapter, the practitioner will be able to:

- Understand infection control
- Understand health and safety issues
- Understand legal and professional issues
- Manage risk, and apply the principles to everyday practice.

Understanding infection control

Healthcare-acquired infections (HAIs) are a major cause of morbidity and mortality among hospitalised patients (Eggiman, Sax & Pittet 2004), with many factors predisposing the patient to the risk of infection. This includes the patient themselves, their environment (particularly when in a hospital environment) and lastly the practitioner's technique. In both venepuncture and intravenous cannulation procedures, the needle used breaches the circulatory system, thus raising the possibility of infection occurring. It is essential that all needles are sterile prior to insertion, especially with cannulation as the device is left in place for a period of time. It is equally important that we use clean personal protective clothing and maintain an aseptic non-touch technique (ANTT) throughout.

Risk to the patient cannot always be reduced as it may often be attributed to their disease (for example, some patients are immunocompromised), the necessary treatment they are receiving (such as chemotherapy or steroids), or their age. The use of antibiotics, invasive procedures or a lengthy stay in hospital can all increase the patient's vulnerability to healthcare-acquired infection.

Environment

To reduce environmental risk, it is important that a clean trolley or tray is used to hold all the equipment you will need. Remember that once a sterile object (such as a needle) comes into contact with a non-sterile one, it will no longer be sterile.

Points for your practice

- **Carefully open sterile packs to ensure that you do not accidentally contaminate them.**

- **If you are in doubt about sterility, treat an item as contaminated.**

- **Don't open sterile packs by an open window or door, as this may cause dust to settle on your sterile objects.**

- **Store your equipment safely to ensure that it does not get damaged.**

- **All the equipment should be inspected prior to use to ensure that it is in date and not damaged. Any equipment that is damaged should be discarded immediately.**

- **Remember, if you are performing venepuncture, blood bottles are not sterile, so you should treat this procedure as 'clean'. Remember to ensure the sterility of your needle though!**

Protective clothing

This is known as personal protective equipment (PPE). Healthcare practitioners must wear disposable gloves at all times during the procedure. Gloves are single-use only. Aprons must also be worn, as there is a risk of blood splashing onto clothing

Hand hygiene

Effective hand washing is essential. Hands should be washed using soap and water, then rinsed, and dried with a disposable paper towel. Clean hands (not visibly soiled) can be decontaminated with an alcohol-based hand rub (or alternative according to your local healthcare provider's policy). Any cuts or abrasions must be covered with a waterproof dressing.

Activity

The National Patient Safety Agency (NPSA) has produced pictorial guidelines showing practitioners how to wash their hands effectively using soap and water or alcohol-based gel. Search out the guidelines on their website (www.npsa.nhs.uk).

Skin preparation

It is important to prepare your patient's skin before undertaking either venepuncture or cannulation. If the skin is visibly dirty, wash it with soap and water to remove any transient flora (Perruca 2001). An antiseptic (such as chlorhexidine 2%) or 70% alcohol-based solution should then be applied for a minimum of 30 seconds (DH 2007). The skin must be allowed to dry for a minute to prevent stinging when the needle pierces and to allow time for disinfection of the site to occur. You must not touch the skin once it has been cleaned. Shaving the site is not recommended prior to cannulation, as damage can be caused to the epithelial layer of the skin. If hair removal is required, the use of clippers or scissors is recommended (RCN 2010).

Other factors that can reduce the risk of infection:

● **Re-siting of cannulas:** The longer a device is in place, the greater the risk of infection. Devices should be replaced every 72–96 hours (RCN 2010) unless there is a valid reason not to do so. If you are leaving a cannula in place longer than the recommended time, ensure that the reasons for this are clearly documented.

● **Replacing IV administration sets:** If you are cannulating a patient to administer medicines or fluids, it is important that IV administration sets (giving sets) are replaced every 72 hours (RCN 2010). The exception to this is for total parenteral nutrition (replace every 24 hours) or blood. Blood-giving sets need changing after every 12 hours, or after each second unit of blood. Ensure that you document on the infusion set the date that it was changed. In between infusion set changes, there should be minimal manipulation of the closed system to avoid the risk of infection entering the site.

● **Dressings:** Ensure that all transparent dressings used are sterile. Check that the packaging is intact before you use a dressing. If it is damaged, discard it. A plaster or dry dressing is usually sufficient to cover the area following venepuncture. For cannulation, a transparent semi-permeable dressing is normally applied so that the cannula site can be regularly observed. Only change the dressing if it is visibly soiled or peeling away from the skin.

● **Tourniquets:** Tourniquets that are soiled with blood are potentially a source of infection, so they should not be used. 'Single use' disposable tourniquets are recommended, but if you use your own elastic tourniquet, ensure that it is cleaned effectively between each patient use.

Understanding health and safety considerations

Sharps

'Sharps' are needles, blades (such as scalpels) and other medical instruments that are necessary for carrying out healthcare work and could cause an injury by cutting or pricking the skin. A sharps injury is an incident in which a sharp penetrates the skin. This is sometimes called a percutaneous injury. These types of injuries are a well-known risk in the health and social care sector.

Sharps contaminated with an infected patient's blood can transmit more than 20 diseases, including hepatitis B and C and human immunodeficiency virus (HIV). Because of this transmission risk, sharps injuries can cause worry and stress to the many thousands who receive them. It is vital that all healthcare staff performing clinical procedures adhere to their local healthcare provider's policies on sharps injuries, and professionally update their knowledge by reading recent evidence-based guidelines.

The EU directive for safer sharps (HSE 2013) makes the following recommendations to prevent sharps injuries from occurring:

● Sharps handling should be kept to a minimum

● Needles must not be bent or broken prior to disposal

● Needles and sharps must not be disassembled prior to disposal

● Needles should not be re-capped

- Used sharps must be discarded into a sharps container at the point of use. Sharps bins must not be filled above two-thirds full (there is a mark on the side of the sharps container indicating the fill line). Containers should not be kept on the floor and should be located in a safe position.

Consider the use of needle-stick prevention devices to provide a safer working environment for practitioners. These need to be evaluated in terms of their effectiveness, cost and benefits before they are introduced across local healthcare settings.

The Health and Safety (sharp instruments in healthcare) Regulations (2013) can be accessed through http://www.hse.gov.uk/ and these are a good source of additional reading on sharps safety.

What to do in the event of a sharps-related injury

All local healthcare providers will have their own procedure to follow in the event of a sharps-related injury (frequently known as a needle-stick injury). It is important that you are aware of what to do if you receive this type of injury.

Always look at your healthcare provider's guidelines to provide you with specific advice for your own area, and follow the steps below:

1. Encourage the wound to bleed and wash it under running water.

2. Report the incident to the manager or person in charge.

3. Report to your Occupational Health Department within 24 hours where possible (allow longer for weekends and bank holidays). They will inform you if your blood and your patient's blood needs taking, if there is a risk of infection to you. To take bloods from your patient, consent will be needed.

4. If you are concerned and your Occupational Health Department is not open, go to your nearest A&E Department (especially if your patient is thought to have Hepatitis or HIV).

5. Once immediate first aid measures have been implemented, ensure that you complete a clinical incident form so that the incident can be recorded. You may be asked to write a statement detailing how the needle-stick injury occurred. Make sure that you document the incident while it is fresh in your memory.

Safety when handling and transporting specimens

You must always take care when handling and transporting specimens. It is important that all specimens are labelled appropriately with the following details:

- Patient's details (name, hospital number, clinical area or GP, date of birth.

- Type of specimen and source taken from (e.g. vein or intravenous device)
- Type of test required, with reason for request
- Time and date of collection
- Signature and printed name of person taking the specimen
- Any potential problems (such as difficulty in bleeding, known risk of infection).

All specimens should be collected in a container that conforms to British standards, one that is strong and leak-proof. Specimen containers should be placed in an individual clear transportation bag and sealed. The blood requisition (request) form is held in a separate part of the specimen bag to avoid contamination should the specimen leak. Once the specimen is placed in the bag, you need to ensure that it is stored safely until it is collected.

Other health and safety considerations

You must have an awareness of your local healthcare provider's policies and procedures in relation to:

- Sharps disposal
- Needle-stick injury
- Disposal of clinical waste
- Checking of medicines and the safe storage of drugs (where appropriate).

Understanding the legal and professional issues

It is our duty to provide our patients with safe and effective care. Medical staff historically performed venepuncture and cannulation. However, more recently these roles have been performed by a wider range of healthcare practitioners and unregistered staff. It is important that you have an awareness of the legal and professional issues that are part of the expanding role and responsibility of the healthcare practitioner. Although this role can increase a professional's knowledge base and skill level, it also carries an increased potential legal risk.

Accountability

Accountability for registered healthcare practitioners is related to the concept of professionalism. Professional regulation through a statutory body (such as the Nursing and Midwifery Council) is required in order to practise professionally. Unregistered healthcare practitioners assume accountability for their practice if they deem themselves as competent and accept the delegated task. A registered practitioner is professionally and legally accountable in four ways:

1. To their regulatory body in terms of their professional code of conduct (with the potential penalty of removal from the register if found in breach of the code of conduct)

2. To the patient through civil law (the practitioner could be sued through the legal system)

3. To the employer through the contract of employment

4. To the public through criminal law (i.e. the sanction could be criminal prosecution)

Under civil law, an individual who has been harmed as a consequence of poor or inadequate care whilst being treated by a registered professional can claim compensation. The claim may be considered as a breach of the individual's duty of care.

Activity

Look up the terms 'accountability', 'duty of care' and 'civil law'. What do they mean in relation to your daily practice?

In terms of accountability in relation to venepuncture and cannulation, you must:

- Be competent to perform the skill
- Have undergone the correct training
- Have undergone a period of supervised practice
- Have been deemed competent by another competent practitioner in order to perform the skill unsupervised
- Be happy to perform the skill
- Recognise your own limitations
- Be willing to re-train if you have not performed the skill for an extended period of time
- Be aware of the legal and ethical issues and update your practice accordingly.

Documentation

Maintaining an accurate record of the procedure is vital in relation to accountability and your own professional practice. Failure to document your interventions accurately could have both legal and professional consequences. Documentation required for legal purposes will be carefully scrutinised, and any failure noted could potentially compromise the individual. The importance of documentation is often overlooked in the healthcare profession, particularly when the workload is high. However, it is worth remembering the saying 'care not documented is care not done' when it comes to writing up your patient records. For cannulation, documentation should include patient consent (and identifying how it was given), the time and date of insertion, the location of the device, the type of cannula and gauge used, the signature, and the printed name and designation of the practitioner inserting the device, as well as any problems encountered during or after the procedure. Regular assessment of the site should also be documented either in the patient's notes or on a cannula care pathway.

For venepuncture, it is important to record the patient's consent (and identify how it was given), which site blood was taken from, the samples taken and any additional problems or complications during or after the procedure. Again, a signature, printed name and designation of the healthcare practitioner are required.

Consent

It is vital that the patient consents to treatment. From the legal and professional perspectives, it is essential that consent be:

- Given by a competent person
- Voluntarily given
- Informed (i.e. full information about the procedure and the risks has been given).

Consent can be given verbally, implied (for example, a patient holds out their arm) or written. The law does not currently require that consent must be given in a particular way; they are all valid methods. However, implied consent should be avoided, as it has no standing in a court of law. It is important that the procedure is fully explained, with the potential risks identified and that the patient can exercise their right to say no. Whichever method of consent is used, it is essential that this be documented in the patient's notes.

Summary

This chapter has highlighted some of the risks that need to be considered when performing either venepuncture or cannulation. You may wish to read additional texts in more detail to gain a deeper understanding, particularly in relation to some of the professional issues. Make sure that you read and adhere to your local healthcare provider's professional code of practice to ensure your own safety.

Appendix 1

Self-assessment checklist for venepuncture to ensure safe practice

Key objective	**YES** (Please tick)	**NO** (Please tick)
Preparation		
The environment has been prepared appropriately prior to undertaking the procedure.		
You have selected the correct equipment to perform venepuncture, including appropriately sized needles and the most suitable blood collection system.		
The patient has been positioned appropriately on a bed or chair, with the limb supported, and is comfortable.		
Assessment of the patient: You have gained informed verbal consent.		
You have accurately assessed the patient's veins, and their general condition.		
You have chosen the most appropriate vein in consultation with the patient and can provide a rationale for the choice.		
The procedure		
You have followed your local healthcare provider's infection control guidelines and adhered to the principles of aseptic non-touch technique (ANTT) when undertaking this procedure.		
You have decontaminated your hands again, and put on gloves and an apron.		
The insertion site has been cleaned and allowed to dry.		
The tourniquet is socially clean (if using a non-disposable tourniquet). A single-use tourniquet is advocated.		
You have adopted an accurate insertion technique:		
The vein has been anchored.		
The needle has been inserted at the correct angle, using a bevel-up approach.		
The blood collection bottles have been filled and changed appropriately (as required).		
The tourniquet has been released at the end of the procedure.		
The puncture site has been cared for, with pressure applied to the site for approximately 2 minutes and a dry dressing applied.		

You have identified and acted upon any problems associated with the procedure.		
All sharps have been disposed of immediately.		
Aftercare		
You have allowed time for the patient to ask questions, to check that they understand care of the puncture site and who to report to in case of any noted problems.		
You have left your patient comfortable and relaxed.		
All clinical waste has been disposed of as per your local healthcare provider's policy.		
All sharps have been disposed of according to your local healthcare provider's policy.		
Samples have been 'inverted' (mixed) immediately after filling for the recommended length of time.		
Blood requisition forms and collection tube labels contain the required patient information.		
You have appropriately recorded and documented all the information about the procedure in the patient's notes or care pathway		

Signature of Learner ....

(Print name) ....

Signature of Assessor ....

(Print name) ....

Date of competency...

Appendix 2

Self-assessment checklist for cannulation to ensure safe practice

Key objective	YES (Please tick)	NO (Please tick)
Preparation		
You have washed your hands prior to the procedure.		
The environment has been prepared appropriately before undertaking the procedure.		
You have selected the appropriate equipment for cannulation, including an appropriately sized cannula. All equipment should be placed on a clean procedure tray/trolley.		
The correct identity of the patient is known and verbal consent has been gained.		
The patient is positioned appropriately on a bed or chair and is comfortable.		
You have explained the procedure thoroughly and gained the patient's consent.		
Assessment of the patient You have accurately assessed the patient's veins, and their general condition.		
Local anaesthetic has been considered (where appropriate) and has been prescribed and applied to the limb.		
The procedure You have followed your local healthcare provider's infection control guidelines and adhered to the principles when undertaking this procedure.		
The insertion site has been cleaned and allowed to dry prior to cannula insertion.		
The tourniquet is socially clean (if using a non-disposable tourniquet). A single-use tourniquet is advocated.		
You have adopted an accurate insertion technique:		
The vein has been anchored.		
The cannula has been inserted 1–2cm into the vein at an angle between 10 and 40 degrees.		
Primary flashback has been observed.		

The cannula has been withdrawn off the stylet and a secondary flashback has been observed.		
The tourniquet has been released.		
Pressure has been applied above the vein tip.		
The injection cap has been applied.		
The cannula has been flushed to ensure patency and an appropriate dressing has been applied.		
Any immediate problems associated with the procedure have been identified and dealt with.		
Aftercare You have allowed time for the patient to ask questions, and they understand how to care for the cannula while it is in place.		
You have left your patient comfortable and relaxed.		
All clinical waste has been disposed of as per your local healthcare provider's policy immediately following the procedure.		
All sharps have been disposed of as per your local healthcare provider's policy.		
You have appropriately recorded and documented all the information in the cannula care pathway, or your patient's notes, including the following information:		
The date and time of insertion		
Type and gauge of device		
Site of insertion		
Your name and job title		

Signature of Learner ....

(Print name) ....

Signature of Assessor ....

(Print name)...

Date of competency...

References

Bland, A. (2008). *Routine Blood Results Explained*. Keswick: M&K Update Publishing.

Campbell, J. (1995). Making sense of venepuncture technique. *Nursing Times*. **91** (31), 29–31.

Davies, S. (1998). The role of nurses in intravenous cannulation. *Nursing Standard*. **11** (2), 47–54.

Department of Health (2001). The Epic Project: developing national evidence based guidelines for preventing healthcare associated infections. London: The Stationery Office.

Department of Health (2007). Saving lives: reducing infection, delivering clean and safe care. High impact intervention 1. Central venous catheter care bundle. London: The Stationery Office.

Department of Health (2010). High impact intervention: peripheral IV cannula care. London: The Stationery Office.

Department of Health (2011). Reducing healthcare associated infections: high impact intervention, blood cultures. London: The Stationery Office.

Dougherty, L. (2000). Changing track on therapy. *Nursing Standard*. **14** (30), 61.

Dougherty, L. (2008). 'Obtaining peripheral access' in Dougherty, L. & Lister, S. (eds). *Intravenous Therapy in Nursing Practice*, 8th edn. Oxford: Blackwell Publishing.

Dougherty, L. (2008). Peripheral cannulation. *Nursing Standard*. **22** (52), 49–56.

Dougherty, L. & Lister, S. (2011). *Royal Marsden Hospital Manual of Clinical Nursing Procedures*, 8th edn. Oxford: Wiley Blackwell.

Dougherty, L. & Watson, J. (2011). 'Vascular access devices' in Dougherty, L. & Lister, S. (2011). *Royal Marsden Hospital Manual of Clinical Nursing Procedures*, 8th edn. Oxford: Wiley Blackwell.

Eggiman, P., Sax, H. & Pittet, D. (2004). Catheter related infections. *Microbes and Infection*. **6** (11), 1033–422.

Ernst, D. (2005). *Applied Phlebotomy*. Philadelphia, USA: Lippincott Williams and Wilkins.

Ernst, D.J. & Ernst, C. (2001). *Phlebotomy for Nurses and Nursing Personnel*. USA: Healthstar Press.

Hadaway, L. & Millam, D. (2005). On the road to successful IV starts. *Nursing*. **35**, 1–14.

Health and Care Professions Council (2008). Standards of conduct, performance and ethics. London: HCPC.

Hefler, L., Grimm, C., Leodolter, S. & Tempfer, C. (2004). To butterfly or to needle: the pilot phase. *Annals of Internal Medicine*. 140 (11), 935–36.

Health and Safety Executive (2013). Health and Safety (sharps instruments in healthcare) Regulations 2013. http://www.hse.gov.uk/pubns/hsis7.htm (last accessed 8.1.14).

Ingram, I. & Lavery, P. (2009). *Clinical Skills for Healthcare Assistants*. Chichester: Wiley Blackwell.

Jackson, A. (1998). Infection control: a battle in vein infusion phlebitis. *Nursing Times*. **94** (4), 68–71.

Lavery, I. (2003). Peripheral intravenous cannulation and patient consent. *Nursing Standard*. **17** (28), 40–42.

Lavery, I. & Ingram, P. (2005). Venepuncture: best practice. *Nursing Standard*. **19** (49), 55–65.

McCall, R. & Tankersley, C.M. (2008). *Phlebotomy Essentials Workbook*. 4th edn. Philadelphia, USA: Lippincott and Williams.

Medical Devices Agency (MDA). (1996). Sterilisation Disinfection and Cleaning of Medical Equipment: Guidance on decontamination from the Medical Advisory Committee to the Department of Health. London: The Stationery Office.

National Patient Safety Agency (NPSA). (2006). Right patient, right blood. Safer practice notice 14. London: NPSA.

Nursing and Midwifery Council (NMC). (2009). Guidelines for records and record keeping. London: NMC.

Nursing and Midwifery Council (2010). The Code: Standards of conduct, performance and ethics for nurses and midwives. London: NMC.

Pearce, L. (2001). Silent epidemic. *Nursing Standard*. **15** (35), 16–17.

Peate, I. & Nair, M. (2011). *Fundamentals of Anatomy and Physiology*. Oxford: Wiley Blackwell.

Perruca, R. (2001). 'Obtaining vascular access' in Hankins, J., Lonsway, R.A.W., Hedrick, C. & Perdue, M.B. (eds). *Infusion Therapy in Clinical Practice*, 2nd edn. Philadelphia: WB Saunders.

Phillips, S., Collins, M. & Dougherty, L. (eds). (2011). *Venepuncture and Cannulation*. Chichester: Wiley Blackwell.

Richardson, R. (ed.) (2008). *Clinical Skills for Student Nurses: Theory, Practice and Reflection*. Exeter: Reflect Press.

Royal College of Nursing (RCN). (2010). *Standards for Infusion Therapy*, 3rd edn. London: RCN.

Scales, K. (2005). Vascular access: a guide to peripheral venous cannulation. *Nursing Standard*. **19** (49), 48–52.

Scales, K. (2008). 'Anatomy and physiology related to intravenous therapy' in Dougherty, L. & Lamb, J. (eds). *Intravenous Therapy in Nursing Practice*, 2nd edn. Oxford: Wiley Blackwell.

Tortora, G. & Derrickson, B. (2011). *Principles of Anatomy and Physiology*. 11th edn. Chichester: Wiley Blackwell.

Ung, L., Cook, S., Edwards, B., Hocking, L., Osmond, F. & Buttergieg, H. (2002). Peripheral intravenous cannulation in nursing: performance predictors. *Journal of Infusion Nursing*. **25** (3), 189–95.

Weinstein, S. (2007). *Plumers principles and practice of intravenous therapy*, 8th edn. Philadelphia, USA: Lippincott, Williams and Wilkins.

Wendler, M.C. (2003). Effects of the Tellington touch in healthy adults awaiting venepuncture. *Research in Nursing and Health*. **26** (1), 40–52.

Witt, B. (2008). 'Vein Selection' in Phillips, S., Collins, M. & Dougherty, L. (eds). *Venepuncture and Cannulation*. Oxford: Wiley Blackwell.

Further reading

Basten, G. (2013). *Blood Results in Clinical Practice*. Keswick: M&K Update Publishing

Bland, A. (2008). *Routine Blood Results Explained*. Keswick: M&K Update Publishing.

Royal College of Nursing (RCN). (2010). *Standards for Infusion Therapy*, 3rd edn. London: RCN.

Index

accountability 80, 81
antecubital fossa 11
anxiety 21, 25
aorta 6
arterial puncture 9, 46, 69
arteries and veins,
    differences between 6, 8, 10
artery, aberrant 14
artery, structure of 8
atrium 6
axillary area 20

basilic vein 14, 16
blood functions 7
blood leakage 68
blood samples 29, 32
blood vessels 7
bruising 46, 74

cannula care pathway 53, 82
cannula, damaged 70
cannula kinking 74
cannula removal 64
cannula, resiting 63
cannula selection 50
cannula tissuing 73
cannulation
    care 53, 54
    complications 67–74
    definition 1
    equipment 52
    reasons for performing 3
    sites for 14, 63
    technique 57–65
    unsuccessful 70
capillaries 7
cephalic vein 14, 15
cerebral vascular accident 20
children 18
circulatory system 5
colour-coding of cannulas 50
competency 2
complications 43, 67
consent 82
contraindications 20

documentation 53, 81, 82
elbow 11
environment 23, 24
environmental risk 76
equipment 23, 29, 52
extravasation 73, 74

fist clenching 22
fluid leakage 70
foot 14, 17
gravity 22

haematoma 44, 69
hand hygiene 77
health and safety 78
heart 6

incomplete blood sample 44, 45
infection control 75, 77
infiltration 73, 74
initial flashback 60, 68
intravenous infusion (IV) 21

legal issues 80

median cubital vein 14, 17
metacarpal veins 14, 17
missing the vein 68

necrosis 73
needle sizes 30
needle-stick injury 79
nerve 46, 69

oedema 20
order of draw 31, 32

pain 47
palpation 19, 21
patient input in choice of vein 19
patient position 21
patient preparation 24
peripheral vascular system 5, 10
phlebitis 47, 71
phlebitis scale 72
phlebotomist 14
preparation 23
protective clothing 76

puncture site care 41

record keeping 52
repeated use of venepuncture/
    cannulation sites 21
right-side heart functions 6
risk reduction 75–82

scars 20
secondary flashback 61, 68
self-assessment 83
septicaemia 71
sharps 78, 79
skin preparation 77
specimens,
    handling and transporting 79
swelling 20

temperature of environment 21
thromboembolism 14
thrombophlebitis 17
tourniquet 22, 24, 30
training 2
tubes for blood samples 32
Tunica Media 9

vacuum system 28, 30, 33
valves 10, 16
vein selection 13, 18, 19
vein stimulation 22
vein, structure of 9
veins, making prominent 22
veins, superficial 16
venepuncture
    complications 43
    definition 1
    devices 28
    problems 43
    reasons for performing 3
    sites for 14
    techniques 27
ventricle 6
visual inspection 19, 21

warming limb 22
winged infusion device 28, 31, 38